The Political Implications of

Soviet Military Power

edited by
Lawrence L. Whetten

Crane, Russak   New York

The Political Implications of Soviet Military Power

Published in the United States of America by
Crane, Russak & Company, Inc.
347 Madison Avenue
New York, New York 10017

Published in Great Britain by
Macdonald and Jane's
(Macdonald and Company (Publishers) Ltd.)
Poulton House, Shepherdess Walk
London N17 LW, Enland

Crane Russak ISBN 0-8448-0910-1
Macdonald and Jane's ISBN 354-01021-2
LC 76-55890

Copyright © 1977 by Crane, Russak & Company, Inc.

Printed in the United States of America

Contents

Preface

The Soviet Union is only just beginning its truly "imperial" phase. Its military forces have acquired intercontinental reach only fairly recently. Its capacity to influence events in remote areas is of relatively recent standing. And it is only just acquiring the habit of defining its interests on a global rather than a solely continental basis.*

In May 1975 an international conference was convened at Ebenhausen, West Germany, under the auspices of the Stiftung für Wissenschaft und Politik and the University of Southern California. The conference was funded by the Thyssen Stiftung, Earhart Foundation and the National Strategy Information Center. The purpose of the conference was to address two fundamental problem areas: (1) the nature of Soviet military power, i.e., difficulties associated with threat perceptions and trend forecasting, changes in doctrine and strategy, modernization of force structures, and future developments in military research and development; and (2) the political utility of Moscow's new military posture.

Papers presented at the conference relating to the first problem area have been published under the title *The Future of Soviet Military Power* by Crane, Russak & Co., New York. The present volume is a compilation of papers dealing with the second topic: the political implications of Soviet military power for the conduct of foreign policy on both the global and regional levels. Soviet policy remains primarily European and American oriented and, accordingly, there are more papers devoted to these areas than to other regions.

* Helmut Sonnenfeldt, Interview in *International Herald Tribune,* 26 January 1976.

Nonetheless, it is essential to preserve a balanced perspective of Soviet world-wide perceptions and three chapters assess Moscow's policies toward its top Asian interests: the Middle East, the Indian Subcontinent and China. Soviet behavior in each region is appraised from the viewpoint of the area's vulnerability to foreign manipulation, newly demonstrated flexibility or change in Soviet policy measured against previously accepted norms for expected behavior, interests and motivation, and the constraints that inhibit Soviet policies and actions. Soviet behavior is also examined within the context of the new concepts of bilateralism with the U.S., of trilateralism with the U.S. and China, and of global détente. Generalizations are suggested about the nature of the Soviet correlation of military power with foreign policy objectives. Finally, several observations are made about the political implications of the Soviet's unprecedented military posture at all levels of international contact or threat.

I wish to express my special gratitude to John Levens and Edward Shannon for assistance provided me in the final preparation of the texts of this volume, and its predecessor, *The Future of Soviet Military Power.*

While there has been a delay in publishing this book and some of the time-sensitive contributions have been overtaken by events, such as the death of Mao and the elections in West Germany, Portugal, and Italy, the authors have treated the material in a sufficiently conceptional manner that their papers remain a worthwhile addition to the literature in the field.

The Political Implications of
Soviet Military Power

Bilateralism and the Political Utility of Soviet Military Power

Lawrence L. Whetten

The purpose of this introductory note is to provide a conceptual framework for the dominant consideration in Soviet foreign policy, i.e., the bilateral special great power relationship with the United States, plus a summary of the political atmospherics prevailing when the papers presented in this book were written.

By many criteria for measuring tactical and strategic weapons, Soviet armed forces are superior in quality and quantity to those of the United States and NATO. The Chairman of the NATO Military Committee, British Admiral Sir Peter Hill-Norton, reported in December 1975 that the weapons modernization rate among Warsaw Pact members was more accelerated than in NATO, and that the Pact now enjoyed asymmetrical advantages over the West in many categories of offensive weapons.[1] The backbone for this superiority in theater forces is the Soviet preponderence in strategic systems. Moscow has approximately five times greater throwweight in its missile forces than the United States and is building a new generation of missiles as replacements for systems regarded as its most modern during SALT I. It has the fastest growing and most modern Navy in the world that will soon have four aircraft carriers and a limited overseas interdiction capability. It has over twice the number of men under arms as the United States and continues to

[1] NATO Press Release, 9 December 1975, and NATO *Newsletter*, January 1975.

1

outpace the United States in investment in military research and development. Thus, Soviet military power has reached parity, if not superiority in some systems, with its chief adversary—the United States. Even without further SALT accords, the USSR will have achieved its primary objective—internationally recognized military equality with the strongest global power.

The correlation of military prowess to political influence is the central dogma in the formation of Soviet foreign policy. Soviet officials continually reaffirm the adage that Moscow's primary concern in the development of its military strategy and capabilities has been the NATO threat and U.S. intentions.[2] Yet the achievement of parity with the United States has both lessened the perception of immediate danger to the USSR and provided the basis for the détente process. It should be emphasized that despite the unprecedented military threat now posed by the Soviet buildup, parity and political equality, in Soviet perceptions, are the vital underpinnings for détente. They could not deal as a political equal with the United States from a position of inferiority.

NATURE OF DETENTE

Probably the most difficult task in estimating the political utility of this new military posture is to determine the nature of the détente process, within which future decisions must be made, and the type of constraints détente is likely to impose on Soviet policy. But a few other terms in contemporary international political life are the subject of as much misunderstanding and confusion as détente. The term is sometimes used to describe a concept, a policy, or a situation. It has different connotations for governments and observers with dissimilar political perspectives, and, over time, even these connotations have been subject to frequent change.[3] Thus, does détente

[2]The consensus most frequently heard is that the Soviet Union's highest priority must be to insure that the next war, unlike the last two, will not be fought on Russian soil. The chief targeting emphasis then, is on damage limitatiot and preemption, if necessary. Interviews in Moscow, 3 December 1975.

[3]Marshall Shulman has observed, "To begin with the term itself (détente) is imprecise and often misleading. Although in its strict sense detente suggests only some reduction of tensions, it is generally used to connote a political rapprochement. In retrospect, we see that even in periods when 'détente' was on everyone's lips, as in 1959 and again in 1963-64, the word had at best a qualified application, since the reduction of tension was accompanied by strenuous Soviet efforts to gain political and military advantages. It seems probable, for example, that the Soviet decision to increase production of intercontinental missiles was made during the post-Cuban 'detente' of 1963-64." "Europe versus Détente," *Foreign Affairs*, (April 1967), p. 398.

now imply mutual great-power acceptance of coexistence à la Khrushchev,[4] genuine political rapprochement, as Kennedy envisioned,[5] normalization in relations on Adenauer's terms,[6] involuntary convergence of interests on major issues of contention,[7] punctual acceptance of the responsibilities of bipolarity (and a combined effort against polycentrism),[8] tacit approval of spheres of preponderant influence,[9] joint acceptance of pluralism and limited adoption of instruments for crisis management,[10] pause or decline in the arms race,[11] opportunism combining a hard and soft stand on various issues to gain greater political advantages,[12] fundamental changes in national goals and character, allowing either or both sides to modify their former views and accommodate the opponent's terms for peace (conversion or capitulation),[13] a new form of moderated hostility since the 1968 Prague crisis,[14] a

[4]Erline Bjol, "The USSR, Détente, and the Future of NATO," *Orbis*, (Spring 1969), pp. 226-35.

[5]Address by President John Kennedy, *Bulletin Department of State*, vol. XLIX, no. 1217 (October 1963), p. 695. In his inaugural address Kennedy presented his axiom on deterrence: "For only when our arms are sufficient beyond doubt can we be certain beyond doubt that they will never be used."

[6]Adenauer insisted that détente was dependent upon basic changes within the USSR, *Erinnerungen*, 1945-53, 1953-55, 1955-59, 1965-66; also Anatole Shub, "The Lessons of Czechoslovakia," *Foreign Affairs*, (January 1969), pp. 272-77.

[7]James Dougherty and J. E. Lehman, Jr., ed., *Arms Control for the Late Sixties*, Van Nostrand Reinhold, (1967), p. xxxv.

[8]Pierre Hassner, "The USSR Since Khrushchev" *Survey*, (Spring 1969), p. 49.

[9]Hedley Bull, "The Scope of Soviet-American Relations and the World Order," no. 66, pp. 102-20; and Bennett Kovrig, "Spheres of Influence; A Reassessment," *Survey*, Winter 1969, pp. 102-20.

[10]Alastair Buchan, *Europe's Futures, Europe's Choices*, Columbia University Press (1969), pp. 56-71, 154-56.

[11]Arthur M. Schlesinger, Jr., *A Thousand Days*, Fawcett, (1967), pp. 831-35. This is the most common interpretation held by the myriad of "general disarmers" since the early 1950s.

[12]Kolkowicz, Roman, "The Warsaw Pact: The Entangling Alliance," *Survey*, Winter 1969, pp. 86-101.

[13]Pierre Hassner, "The Implications of Change in Eastern Europe for the Atlantic Alliance," *Orbis*, Spring 1969, p. 243; also Bjol, *Orbis*, Spring 1969, p. 229. On the difficulties of East-West convergence on social and ideological matters see contributions by Melvin Croan and Tiber Szamuely, "The USSR Since Khrushchev," *Survey*, Spring 1969; and Hassner's observation that the main form of convergence is the convergence of worries (*Ibid*).

[14]Philip Windsor has written, "Whereas the détente was previously identified with the status quo, the status quo is now (since Prague) identified with increased hostility. . . . Instead of seeking as far as possible to preserve the status quo in order 'to give détente a chance,' it has now become necessary to accommodate change if the détente is to be secured. And yet there are no indications so far that any government is at e,

complacent acceptance of the status quo,[15] the recognition of a new stability in world order that is mutually beneficial to preserve,[16] an acknowledgment of an inescapable momentum toward détente, and dynamic revisionism propagated mainly by smaller states,[17] or a commitment to great-power immobilism by ignoring rather than resolving disputes?[18]

The aggregation of these views has led to a broad Western interpretation of the concept.[19] Both adversaries are competing to extend their influence in selected areas and have grievances about the constraints some previous commitments have imposed on their policy options. Yet, both have declined the temptation to exploit continuing international tensions to the permanent detriment of the rival. The great powers have adopted a policy of mutually exploring the opponent's values, tolerance levels, relative priorities, probable constraints, and his calculations of possible profits and losses for given decisions. Accordingly, margins of error, uncertainty, and risk have been cautiously identified on specific issues. This entire process of communication and education has aided in uncovering issues of mutual interest, in resolving some conflicting interests, and in establishing the parameters of immediate values.

A deliberate mutual decision to explore areas of accommodation during periods of persisting tension and distrust may be defined as a détente policy. The purpose of this policy, as exercised presently by the great powers, is not only to help reduce tensions and strengthen stability. It is a conscious effort to seek the resolution of those contentious points that are in part responsible for the tensions. For example, both powers have agreed to shift such issues as space exploration and nuclear energy from the contentious or competitive

---

or willing to work for positive changes in East-West relations. . . . Soviet-American relations might continue to develop, but all that can be expected in Europe for the present is at best immobilism, at worst hostility. "The Boundaries of Detente," *The World Today*, June 1969, pp. 257-58.

[15]From Cuba to Prague, "The détente was generally assumed to be identical to the status quo," *Ibid.*, p. 255. Hassner argues that the great powers are presently advocating neither status quo nor revisionist policies at the exclusion of the other. "Change and Security in Europe, Parts I & II," *Adelphi Papers*, nos. 45 and 49, International Institute for Strategic Studies, London.

[16]Curtin Winsor, Jr., "The Nonproliferation Treaty: A Step Toward Peace," *Orbis*, Winter 1969, p. 1015.

[17]Pierre Hassner, "The USSR since Khrushchev," *Survey*, Spring 1969, pp. 45-50.

[18]Philip Windsor, *Germany and the Management of détente*, Chatto and Windus, (1971).

[19]"The Imperative of Peaceful Coexistence," statement by Henry A. Kissinger before the U.S. Senate Foreign Relations Committee, 19 September 1974.

to the cooperative side of the ledger. Such deliberate actions may necessitate an alteration of attitudes and priorities, but not of principles and ultimate values. A *détente policy*, then, is a means, not an end in itself. Initially it requires that both powers gradually identify their respective national interests and aims in terms of reducing opportunities for adversary exploitation and profit, rather than seeking ideological conquests. *Détente process*, then, may be defined as a continuing interaction in which the participants intend to foster a limited degree of adversary cooperation in a nonbellicose atmosphere that is issue-oriented rather than principle — or value-oriented. They also seek "normalcy" in adversary relations as the pragmatic extension of influence on important national interests. A circumscribing feature of the détente process is that it will remain largely limited to issues only and will not generally extend to values.

The Soviets have a slightly different perception of détente. With the emerging U.S.-Chinese rapprochement, Moscow must now calculate the impact of any détente measure with the West on its relations with China and Eastern Europe. Soviet decisions about stability and détente are likely to be even more deliberate than in the past, both because of the uncertainty of allied reactions, and the magnitude of moves now necessary to delineate further the normalization process. This insecurity and uncertainty place specific and absolute limits on the degree of Soviet engagement with the West. As presently constituted, the Soviet model for socialist development cannot accept ideological coexistence or free ideological competition with the West. Until the legitimizing process is complete, ideology will remain the indispensable instrument for justifying continued one party rule and the perpetuation of Communist authority.

The Soviets do not have a word or expression identical to the Western understanding of the term détente. The Soviet conceptualization of this process is known as peaceful coexistence. The concept of peaceful coexistence is a mandate for the continued advancement of the socialist revolution. The economic, political, and ideological aspects of the struggle are to be assertively pursued. Only those policies that might lead to a great-power military confrontation are proscribed. The present Soviet leaders no longer insist that war is inevitable between the two systems, and they are confident that without the chaos of a general war the aggregation of historical forces will dictate the inevitable domination of Socialism. From this basic position two stereotyped interpretations of the present détente atmosphere have been voiced. One consistent theme is that détente is a result of the moral, political and military decline in the West. The changing nature of world forces in favor of the Soviet Union is the result of the growing economic and military power of the USSR in comparison with the West.[20]

The second theme is that ideological warfare must be sharpened to preserve the benefits of Socialism. Brezhnev, for example, specifically reminded the Soviet people after the 1972 Summit Conference of the importance of ideological vigilance.

> We approached the Soviet-American summit talks . . . from positions affirming the principle of peaceful coexistence of states. . . . In striving for the affirmation of the principle of peaceful coexistence, we realize that successes in this important area in no way signify [sic] the possibility of relaxing the ideological struggle. On the contrary, we must be prepared for this struggle to be intensified, for it to become an increasingly crucial form of the confrontation between the two social systems. We have no doubt about the outcome of this confrontation, since the truth of history and objective laws of social development are on our side.[21]

SOVIET POWER IN A CHANGING INTERNATIONAL SYSTEM

The purpose of the Soviet military build-up and the nature of détente have become increasingly ambiguous as the international system in which they are to be applied undergoes fundamental economic and political changes. The ultimate scope of these changes, and the role the USSR will play in shaping them remain hazy. By the nature of its economic system and its non-convertible currency, for example, it can participate only marginally in the remodeling of the world's financial structures.[22]

The vast bulk of the world's nations are demanding that the international system shift its priorities; from preserving peace and promoting the peaceful

[20]Svetlov, B., "USSR-USA: Possibilities and Realities," *International Affairs*, February 1972; also V. Osipov, *Izvestia*, 17 February 1973; and F. D. Kulakov, *Pravda*, 22 April 1972.

[21]*Pravda*, 28 June 1972. For a typical statement of the increasing number of West Europens who are expressing apprehensions about the utility of ideological competition see Theo Summer, "Entspannung hat ihren Preis," *Die Zeit*, 21 September 1973, and the exchange of toasts between Brezhnev and French President d'E'staing in *Survival*, Feb.-Jan. 1976.

[22]The Soviets' chief brake on permanent world inflation is to peg prices at an average of the world market price for the previous five years. This arbitrary device is helpful when selling shoddy industrial goods, but it is also a penalty in marketing many raw materials. For example, it incorporates the present political price of oil, but over the long term, the Soviets will argue, it proves both equitable and deflationary. Interviews, December 1975, Moscow.

settlement of disputes to stimulating economic development and obviating the existing inequalities in material conditions for all humanity. This shift is now occurring. Greater stress is now being placed on global equity than on sustained growth in productivity. These are order of magnitude changes, in both processes and values, which have already run counter to traditional Western societal principles. The changing emphasis of world priorities from security to economic matters has partially accounted for the reordering of the high tension issues from the East-West. to the North-South and West-West arenas; areas where it will be difficult for the Soviets to apply their military power or their own economic model for development.[23]

Accompanying these economic changes, however, is the phenomenon of a new political awakening and mass mobilization. Zbigniew Brzesinski has observed the following:

> Unlike the initial phases of the Industrial Revolution, when the way people lived tended to change more rapidly than how they thought, today—because of mass communication and education—the way people think is changing more rapidly than how they live. All this makes for higher political awareness, increasingly focused on the desire to eliminate the enormous disparaties in the global standard of living.[24]

It is within this phenomenon of new political awareness and rising expectations that the Soviets have the greatest opportunity for translating their military power into political initiative and influence. It would be unwise, however, to suggest that the shift in global priorities from strategic deterrence to income distribution has altered longstanding Soviet military threat perceptions, as mentioned above. But, political mobilization as the result of the economic confrontation adds another dimension for the possible application of Soviet military power.

The political utility of Soviet power, then, should be assessed within the context of both the special great power relationship, a unique arrangement in which the respective perceptions can be aired, and that is now sufficiently broad to afford a variety of levers to influence the opponent, and

[23]Of course, the Soviets do not agree and insist that the present changes favor their long sought goal of a world economy, centrally planned in Moscow. Interviews, 5 December 1975, Moscow. See also Elizabeth Dridd Valkenier, "New Trends in Soviet Economic Relations," *World Politics,* April 1970; and Marshall I. Goldman, *Soviet Economic Aid,* (1967).

[24]Zbigniew Brzezinski. "The Changing World System," *New York Times,* reprinted *International Herald Tribune,* 10 October 1975; see also his "Recognizing the Crisis," *Foreign Policy,* Winter 1974-75.

within the specific nature of the localized issue. Thus, all local crises or problems, including third parties, should be treated on at least two levels of perception; analysis and diplomacy within great-power bilateralism, and at the local or regional level. Determining the linkage and the degree of consultation and cooperation practiced between these levels of analysis will contribute to the interpretation of the nature and scope of the Soviet commitment to the détente process.

CONSTRAINTS AND OPPORTUNITIES IN SOVIET FOREIGN POLICY

While outsiders have little specific knowledge about the Soviet decision-making process, there is enough evidence from final actions and public literature indicating that constraints, ranging from intellectual dissent to grain shortages, influence the conduct of Soviet foreign policy. These constraints have been analyzed individually in great depth by Western scholars, but the principal factors converged for a variety of largely fortuitous reasons before the 25th Soviet Communist Party Congress in February 1976 over the issue of political leadership and the impending succession crisis.

Throughout 1975 there were widespread rumors about the imminent resignation of Party chief Brezhnev, the Soviets' primary supporter of détente, at or soon after the Party Congress. Events now identified with the presuccession struggle within the Kremlin shed light on the constraints within the bureaucracy, the varying Soviet interpretations of peaceful coexistence, and the applications of military power within the context of perceived opportunities and imposed constraints.

World events made the timing of Brezhnev's replacement seem propitious. The United States had withdrawn from Southeast Asia after the North Vietnamese victory, opening the region to the expansion of Soviet influence. Initiatives by the United States in the Middle East had solved marginal matters but had again been stymied on central issues that were not likely to be settled without more active Soviet involvement. SALT I had led to SALT II talks, where the Soviets retained valuable chips in the size, throwweight and versatility of their missile forces. A final agreement was expected that would preserve these Soviet advantages. The Conference on Security and Cooperation in Europe (CSCE), which the Soviets had long championed, had culminated with a European summit conference in Helsinski and a Final Act defining levels of cooperation and interaction. Correspondingly, the U.S.-sponsored negotiations on military disengagement (MBFR) had been effectively placed on the back burner. (See Chapter 2.) In economic matters, the West was suffering the worst economic depression since World War II. The "crisis of capitalism," as the Soviets asserted, had important political side-effects, especially in Southern Europe. The Cypress dispute and the sharp deterioration in Turkish-American relations provided opportunities to advance Soviet interests, which Moscow readily accepted by Kosygin's visit in December 1975 to Ankara. Italy's thirty-seventh governmental crisis in thirty-nine years again raised the spectre, in 1976, of a Communist-Christian Democratic coalition. The death of Spain's General Franco triggered widespread labor and political unrest and created profound uncertainties about the country's future. Finally, Portugal had suffered two years of political upheaval that had left the country in virtual chaos and ripe for extremist actions. With the "crisis in capitalism" and the dilemma of political legitimization facing Southern Europe, Brezhnev sought an all-European Communist Party Conference to establish a concerted effort for the advancement of Socialism.

OPPORTUNITIES CUM CONSTRAINTS

The capstone to this favorable progression of events registering the accomplishments of the decade-long Brezhnev rule was apparently to have been the appointment of a successor, representing the first instance of the transition of power in Soviet history when the incumbent voluntarily left office. But by mid-1975 the Kremlin had adopted policies of deliberate assertion in Africa, the Indian Ocean, and Southeast Asia, cool reservation toward leading Arab countries and China, and an increasingly intransigent bargaining position at SALT, MBFR talks, and on legal issues related to West Berlin.

Unforeseen developments had impaired the juggernaut of Brezhnev's expectations. The U.S. withdrawal from Southeast Asia opened the area to both Soviet and Chinese influence, with the latter fairing better than expected. Peking opened diplomatic relations with other Asian countries, including India, and made inroads into Cambodia and Thailand. Relations with Vietnam were marred over rival territorial claims to the potentially oil-rich and strategically important Paracel and Spratley islands. Hanoi maintained a balanced position, however, by rejecting Moscow's repeated call for an Asian security conference. Brezhnev's aims for full participation in the Middle East

nt process appeared to be more long range than immediate. He had
ancelled a state visit to Egypt that would have paralleled Nixon's trium-
our, because of deteriorating relations between the two countries. He
also lost the initiative on the Palestinian question to the Syrians. The
SALT II negotiations had resolved the verification question for "MIRVing"
Soviet missiles by consigning types of missiles flight-tested with MIRVs to the
allotted 1300 missile ceiling agreed to at Vladivostok. But the United States'
inexpensive low-level-penetration cruise missile, capable of launch from submarines, aircraft, or surface ships, with ranges of up to 2000 miles, was
used by the United States as a bargaining counter for the imposition of constraints on the Soviet's Backfire bomber. Sufficient acrimony had built up in
the United States over SALT that almost any agreeement would be subject
to criticism, especially during an election year. SALT II could no longer
serve its original political goal as the culminating symbol of a "generation
of peace." (See Chapter 9.)

At the CSCE Conference, the Soviets had achieved only their minimum
objectives of gaining international recognition of the political boundaries of
Eastern Europe. In "basket one," they finally agreed to a detailed charter to
reduce the prospects of surprise attack in Europe by distinguishing between
military actions perceived as precautionary moves and those that were
clearly provocative. In exchange for the technology sought in "basket two,"
Moscow was forced to recognize the West's terms for peaceful change within
the Soviet system, and that the West would continue to promote social evolution in East Europe. The problem remains to find an acceptable formula for
modernization that will accommodate the intellectual spin-off of technological
improvements and the West's emphasis on individuality with the Soviet's ideological tolerance levels that stress common will and collective benefits. Likewise MBFR presented no panaceas for durable European stability. Western
members, and finally the United States, recognized that the political climate
was changing and that an early military disengagement, however small,
could now have an adverse euphoric effect on world opinion. Thus, the pressure for agreement was substantially relaxed and overall expectations had
been reduced. From the Western view, moreover, the consultations among
the NATO members had become one of the most positive contributions to
alliance cohesion in its history and, therefore, partially justified continuing
the talks.

In economic matters, the USSR suffered in 1975 one of its worst years
since World War II. Chairman of the State Planning Commission and

Deputy Prime Minister Nikolai K. Baibakov announced in the annual economic statement to the Supreme Soviet that industrial growth in 1975 was 7.5 percent, down from the original Five Year Plan of 8.8 percent. Overall industrial growth for 1976 was pegged at a mere 4.3 percent because of shortages in agricultural raw materials. Heavy industry is to increase 4.9 percent in 1976, but consumer industry is planned to grow at only 2.7 percent. National income in 1975 rose only 4 percent against the Five Year Plan goal of 7.4 percent. In 1976 it is programmed to rise by 5.4 percent.[25]

Agriculture was the hardest hit, mainly because of drought. Planned grain production was to be 215.6 million tons, but only an estimated 135 million tons were actually harvested. A disastrous 70 million tons shortfall (or one-third the planned total) that depleted limited reserves, compelled massive grain imports and curtailed expansion of livestock herds. By December 1975, the USSR had bought 20 million tons of grain from the United States and large amounts of barley, wheat, corn, and soybeans from Spain, Brazil, Rumania, and Argentina. Under strong U.S. pressure to regulate grain exports and reduce domestic inflation. Moscow agreed, in an unprecedented step, to purchase at least 30 million tons of grain from the United States over a five year period, on terms favorable to U.S. shippers.[26] At the same time Moscow was seeking massive Western technological infusion. As a result, Foreign Trade Minister Nikolai Patolichev announced that the total Soviet trade turnover for 1975, which included COMECON, was expected to be up 20 percent over the previous year to $60 billion.[27] Still the Soviet trade deficit with four leading Western industrial nations during the first six months of 1975 exceeded $5.0 billion.

While Soviet imports of both grain and technology-intensive industrial products increased sharply, exports of raw materials to Eastern Europe averaged only half the world market price, and exports to the West generally fell because of reduced demands for primary products (Western European oil imports during 1975 dropped one million tons). The consequence was

[25]TASS, 3 December 1975. The projected figures for the new 1976-1980 Five Year Plan were substantially below those of the previous Plan in most categories, with the exception of such export items as oil, which was expected to rise from 25-30 percent, or from 490 million tons (making the USSR the world's leading producer) to 620-640 million tons; *New York Times*, 15 December 1975. See Marshall I. Goldman, "The Soviet Economy is Not Immune," *Foreign Policy*, Winter 1975-76.

[26]*New York Times*, 4 and 10 December 1975.

[27]TASS, 3 September 1976. Japan increased its exports to the USSR 143 percent in first six months of 1975, and the United States enjoyed a 4 to 1 advantage in trade with Russia during the same period.

that the USSR was compelled for the first time since World War II to seek major credits and loans from the West.[28]

COMMUNISM IN DISARRAY

However serious the Kremlin's present economic plight is, it is likely to be transitory, and impart only a temporary impact on détente. A more critical foreign policy issue for the durability of détente is the Kremlin's campaign for the convocation of an all-European Communist Conference to be followed by a World Communist Conference; complete with the polemical debate it will release within the Soviet Union and elsewhere in the Communist World. The conferences were originally to be held before the 1976 25th CPSU Party Congress, and the initial consultative meeting of the 28 European parties was held in October 1974 in Warsaw. The independent parties (mainly the Italian, Spanish, British, Swedish, Yugoslav, Rumanian, and later the French) insisted upon adoption of the principle of decision-making by consensus, which insured them a veto and favorable prospects for confining the conference to the non-ideological matters of peace and security in Europe. The consensus rule stimulated interparty debates on the crisis in the West, peaceful versus forceful acquisition of power, and the impact of revolution on coexistence.

The debate was publicly launched by Central Committee Secretary B. N. Ponomarev in the January 1975 issue of *Problems of Peace and Socialism*, and by A. I. Sobolev in the January 1975 issue of *The Working Class and the Contemporary World*. The authors argued that the thrust of Communism should be intensified against the Western world because of opportunities provided by the crisis of capitalism, the stability of détente, and the mutual deterrence of nuclear parity. In the April 1975 issue of *Problems of Peace and Socialism*, the editor Konstantin Zarodov, argued that the class struggle in the West had changed in character, and he questioned whether the ballot box was merely "waiting interminably for revolution" and therefore irrelevant to proletarian internationalism. On 6 August, *Pravda* printed a similar article by Zarodov. The debate over revolution against demoralized capitalist societies had reached such proportions that Brezhnev himself felt

[28]By November the figure discussed in London had reached 200 million pounds. Interviews, staff members, *Financial Times*, London, 28 November 1975. The domestic impact of this strained economy is that a "counter economy" now openly flourishes, dealing in everything from Western short-wave radios to apartments and even Moscow residence permits and an open housing market.

compelled to take sides by personally receiving Zarodov and publicly praising his work (*Pravda*, 18 September 1975). On 23 September the lead editorial in *Pravda* criticized the Zarodov line, and the debate over "revolution now" appeared increasingly in party organs and academic journals.[29]

The impact of the debate on the Western Communist Parties was soon apparent. The Spanish delegate to the November 1975 consultative meeting for the European conference complained that parties which had earlier wanted the conference before their party congresses (CPSU) were now advocating postponement.[30] A Soviet commentator then called for a "principled, militant, Marxist-Leninist final (conference) document which should also be a general conclusion for all Communists in their struggle for European peace, security, cooperation, and social progress."[31] Yugoslav media commentators publicly charged Brezhnev by name with attempting to use the conference to restore Soviet discipline over the European Communist parties and thereby "opening, or rather deepening, a new crisis among individual Communist parties." [32] The Secretary-General of the Spanish Communist Party, Santiago Carrillo, defined the crisis in these terms:

> There cannot be a line [meaning firm linkage, L.W.] between the communist parties of the capitalist countries and the state parties of Eastern Europe. There cannot be a global strategy. If there were one, the principle of coexistence as noninterference in the affairs of others would be violated, because that would mean giving, not just to another communist party, but to another state, the possibility of interfering in our affairs and having a voice in our strategy.[33]

Later he stated that "the old internationalism is a historical residue, destined

[29]See particularly *International Life, The Working Class and the Contemporary World,* and *Problems of Peace and Socialism.*

[30]RFE Research Background Report, 176-177, 16 and 18 December 1975.

[31]TASS, 10 December 1975; also Rude Pravo, 10 December 1975 called for a "really militant communist document."

[32]Radio Zagreb, 15 and 10 December 1975. The commentator was referring specifically to Brezhnev's statement that, "The socialist community is an alliance of an absolutely new type. It . . . represents a fraternal family of peoples . . . which are forged into a single whole by a *common world outlook,* common lofty ideals and relations of comradely solidarity and mutual support." TASS, 9 December 1975 (italics supplied). See also W. E. Butler, "Legal Configurations of Integration—in Eastern Europe," *International Affairs,* October 1975. In a related matter, many Yugoslavs privately link the rash of anti-government plots in the latter half of 1975 that were officially labelled Soviet-sponsored were tied both to the Kremlin succession crisis and to Yugoslav resistance in the consultative meeting for the European Communist Conference.

[33]Quoted in RAD 177, 18 December 1975.

to disappear." He also advocated restructuring internationlism along lines
of Western and Eastern European priorities, and stated that the conference
could now only take place if conducted on a nonideological basis.[34] The conference was held under these limitations in June 1976.

PRE-SUCCESSION CRISIS

The ongoing debate over militancy versus peaceful coexistence indicated that
the Kremlin's authority over its staunchest supporters in capitalist societies
was waning and reflected the general hardening of Soviet policy in related
areas. These trends led to speculation about the state of the Soviet collective
leadership, namely that: (1) the pro-détente Brezhnev faction was losing its
authority and was less confident about the long term personal political advantages derived from pursuing détente; (2) the collective was fissuring into
rival factions without discernible leaders and whose coalition loyalties were
shifting with issues; (3) Brezhnev had been a master consensus politician,
building unanimity before extending personal commitment or wielding cha-
risma—no other Politburo member could match these qualities without the full
authority of his position.[35] Indeed all three possibilities may have characterized Kremlin leadership difficulties at the time.

The new assertiveness in the wake of the unprecedented presuccession

34While visiting West Germany in 1975, Carrillo insisted that there was not only
no common line, but vehemently condemned the Portuguese Communist Party violation
of a previous agreement among Italian, Spanish, French and Portuguese Communist
Parties not to resort to force.

35It has also been asserted that during the same period the other great powers, the
United States and China, were experiencing similar presuccession troubles. Traditional
election year campaign problems in the United States were accompanied by a series of
Chinese overtures to both Moscow and Washington suggesting a bid to keep Peking's
options open for the post-Mao phase. After Lin Piao's death, Chou-En-lai felt less
constrained in seeking some adjustment with Moscow that could match progress with
the United States. In 1973, while border negotiations were still in progress, Chou
publicly asked Moscow for some sign of good faith. In 1974 he sent a congratulatory
message on the October Revolution anniversary and accepted the Soviet offer of a
nonaggression treaty, which was rejected as insincere by the USSR. In January 1975,
China again asked for some small gesture, first before visits by Kissinger, then President
Ford, and finally, Nixon's daughter. Throughout the year China quietly dropped its campaign for the return of Taiwan. In the most obvious political move yet toward the USSR,
in December 1975 Peking released the Soviet helicopter crew held for twenty months
with "conclusive" proof of espionage, on grounds of "insufficient" evidence. Thus there
was discernible policy flux in all three capitals (the least being in Washington and
possibly the most in Moscow, where the succession procedures are the least predictable—China has appointed a Vice Chairman who will presumably serve until the next
Party Congress). For an excellent discussion of the Chinese succession question and

crisis also signalled that the policy reversals and resulting factionalism were sufficiently grave that the succession question would have to be delayed until a more opportune time, or until death intervened. In the interim, factionalism and personal rivalry could increase the trend toward assertiveness in foreign policy and the application of dual standards in the practice of coexistence. Paradoxically, the aggregation of constraints culminating in the succession crisis did not generate indecision or pacifity. Rather, it reflected the continuity in the Soviet political elite which, under the temporary stress of factionalism, underwent an involuntary, but necessary, reversion to previously disregarded Marxist-Leninist norms for capitalist-socialist competition as a lowest-common-denominator-compromise. The result was a strengthening of Soviet interest in the acceleration of integration in Eastern Europe, a more active commitment to the revolutionary cause in the West, and a deeper engagement in Third World affairs—a dual standard asserting that the status quo, when favorable, and socialist progression, when possible, must be acknowledged by the West ("coexistence implies no ban on class struggle").

LEADERSHIP AND FOREIGN POLICY OPTIONS

The succeeding faction in the leadership struggle, regardless of the personalities included, will undoubtedly perpetuate the "permanently operating factors" that have guided Soviet policy during the Brezhnev period.[36] These include: (1) continuation of the undivided authority of a Soviet Communist Party with its traditional methods of Party control (relaxation would encourage intrigue); (2) strengthening the centralized nature of the regime both to insure administrative control and to exercise the Russian concept of *vlast*, the willingness to demonstrate power for preventive or deterrent political purposes; (3) preservation of a satisfactory relationship among the Party, the armed forces, and the security forces, which means perpetuating the present class structures with existing elites; (4) the expansion of economic growth through importing Western technology and stimulating local innovation.

Whomever Brezhnev's successor is, and however he attains power, he

---

the presumed instability until after de-Maoization see Thomas Robinson, "Political Succession in China," *World Politics,* October 1974.

[36]This interpretation was born out by recent interviews with East German officials. When asked who would follow Brezhnev, their reply was, "Brezhnev." Interviews, November 1975, East Berlin.

will probably gain the agreement of his senior colleagues to close ranks with him and project the image of collective leadership necessary to insure the elites that an orderly succession has been achieved. But, because of the age of the leading contenders (Andrei Kirilenko is 69) the new regime will be a "caretaker administration" until younger blood can provide more durability (indeed, it may require more than one interim government). Furthermore, there is no assurance that Brezhnev's successors will try or will be able to emulate Brezhnev's style of leadership; rivalries may prompt harsher repression.[37]

Brezhnev avoided the mistakes Khrushchev made with the Party apparatus, military high command, industrial managers, and foreign policy. Accordingly, he became relatively predictable and deliberately preserved the shroud of collectivity. The available evidence suggests that the Soviet leaders experienced uncertainty and may have sought latitude to test their individual notions and to demonstrate their respective leadership abilities during the presuccession phase. The threat of uncertainty alone will be strong inducement among the top elite to avoid confusion, ambiguity, and excessive opportunism, and to opt for stability, even if it means risking greater predictability.

The present ambiguity between the continuity of the ruling elite and the growing rivalry of its leading figures suggests that a new phase may be emerging in the Soviet interpretation of coexistence. Or it may suggest that the special great-power relationship is likely to be the governing factor in Moscow's political use of its military power. Coexistence cannot be totally abandoned or even seriously impaired without risking nuclear war and jeopardizing the "gains of socialism." The correlation between military power and political objectives is likely to remain a constant consideration for Soviet leaders, but the practice of coexistence may become increasingly adroit as the Soviets seek an ever widening variety of foreign policy options.

CONCLUSION

It is now generally recognized that global détente or peaceful coexistence is motivated neither by a desire to promote convergence nor *entente* of

[37]A comparison between the leadership styles of Brezhnev and Khrushchev is in Sidney Ploss, "New Politics in the USSR," *Survey*, Autumn 1973. Kulakov (age 57), Central Committee Secretary seems the most likely long term successor to Brezhnev, and Mazurov (age 67) a likely replacement for Kosygin. For a general treatment see Myron Rush, *How Communist States Change Their Rulers*, Cornell University Press, 1974.

rival societal aims or political interests. National objectives among rival states will remain competitive. States will continue to seek political influence, achieved in the past by exploiting a rival's vulnerability on the entire spectrum of contentious issues. More than ever before, influence-competition is based on military balances, either on global or regional levels. The challenge of the new era is to determine how influence-competition can be sufficiently temporized to dampen or control military arms racing which might upset the existing balances.

The Soviet concept of peaceful coexistence apparently is undergoing a substantial change. Under Khrushchev it was the rationale for promoting Soviet state interests by any means short of war. Now the concept has become far more elaborate. It requires the attainment and preservation of military parity at any level of prospective violence or political challenge. For the Soviets, parity has become a national imperative of the highest order. The issue at the arms control negotiations with the Americans and Europeans has been not merely to establish physical ceilings that will guarantee or institutionalize parity, but, additionally, to insure that military equivalence, includes both options and constraints in pursuing national objectives. From the West's viewpoint, constraints against waging war must be accompanied by restraints against exploiting opportunities to expand political influence that could generate suspicions and tensions. Thus the "struggle for parity," to use the Soviet term, must be linked to a balance of constraints, as seen by the West.

The USSR has participated with other states in attempting to characterize this equivalence in restraints by defining norms for political behavior (as in the 1972 "Basic Principles" and in the CSCE Final Act signed in 1975). But, agreeing to operational codes of conduct, rules for greater exchange of technology and freer flow of information has not solved the Soviet's fundamental problem of how to insure reciprocity in constraints while promoting the goals of Socialism. They have not satisfactorily answered the question of whether their aims should be to seek individual advantages over rivals, promote mutual gains, or advance pluralistic benefits (something for everyone). Is the traditional concept of the "correlation of historic forces for the progression of socialism" still a zero-sum game in which the gains for Socialism represent corresponding losses for its opponents? Or, can these forces now be interpreted so that Soviet state interests can be protected without necessarily reducing a rival's options? There is no means of enforcing norms, channeling behavior, or institutionalizing options. Reciprocity remains the most viable instrument for influencing an opponent's actions. There is no assurance that misperceptions, inaccurate estimations, and unwise decisions will not trigger responses in kind from an adversary. Yet the danger of over-reaction will remain one of the underpinnings of the prudence and caution that characterizes the new balance of constraints.

The Soviets are unlikely to seek a theoretical definition or formal codification of national objectives. "Excessive cooperation" with other states will be averted whenever possible as an infringement on the nebulous "correlation of historic forces." Yet the Soviet Union is deliberately enhancing its stake in preserving the stability of the international system itself, especially in high priority regions and in the various special relationships it is cultivating. This increased Soviet interest in systemic stability has been regarded in the West as a second feature of the overall balance of constraints. Finally, should the Soviets become more issue-oriented and less ideologically motivated in foreign policy, the benefits of the on-going bargaining process itself may be recognized as adequate compensation for the acceptance of specific constraints. Thus, the Soviets can be expected to maximize and exploit opportunities to expand their political influence, but there are inhibiting factors that Soviet decision-makers are unlikely to disregard. Soviet military power is most likely to be applied between the two extremes of opportunities imparting low political risks and constraints with minimal flexibility.

Soviet Foreign and Defense Policy: A Global View

Malcolm Mackintosh

INTRODUCTION

The main aim of this paper is to take a look at Soviet political and military aims and objectives as they are probably seen from Moscow by the group of men who have governed the Soviet Union for the last twelve years. Soviet foreign and defense policies form part of an evolutionary process; they are much involved with military and economic factors, and many of their roots are to be found in Russian history, and some in the current phase of Soviet Communist thinking. We are taking a look at a process which is developing all the time. Therefore, while some of the points to be raised here are constant factors, many are liable to change. Much of the Soviet activity in the field of foreign policy is opportunistic in the way in which it is carried out, and is therefore difficult to assess, let alone predict with any degree of accuracy.

THE SOVIET LEADERSHIP

Since we want to look at Soviet aims through Soviet eyes, it may be worthwhile considering whose eyes we are borrowing for this purpose. The present Soviet leadership, composed mostly of men in their late sixties or early seventies, has been in power since October 1964—over a decade. The leading figures, Brezhnev, Kosygin, and Podgorny, together with Kirilenko and Mazurov, were brought up in the Stalin era, rose to eminence under Khrushchev, whom they overthrew in a Palace revolution in 1964, and have maintained a remarkably stable relationship (at least on the surface) among themselves since then.

There have been relatively few changes in the ruling Politburo, to which new voting members have been appointed on a carefully arranged system of checks and balances to ensure that no one leader achieves total domination of the Party. This applies even after the 1973 additions under which Foreign Minister Gromyko and Defense Minister Marshal Grechko were made members of the Politburo, along with Andropov, the head of the KGB. The Politburo now consists of fifteen Party and Communist leaders, each of whom, broadly speaking, is responsible for one or more of the major aspects of Soviet life today. Within the Politburo, Brezhnev enjoys primacy, but not dominating power, in a leadership which is still basically collective.

Brezhnev is an experienced, cautious, and hard-headed Party administrator, deeply convinced of the greatness of the Soviet Union and of the correctness of current Party doctrine. He is strongly nationalistic and conscious that it is he and his colleagues who have brought the Soviet Union through its final stages from great-power to superpower states. Yet he is the heir of many traditional Russian and up-to-date Soviet beliefs and convictions. Among these are: (1) the need to avoid war with the other superpower, the United States; (2) the special role of preeminence which Russia ought to play in Europe; (3) the very basic fear and dislike of China, and to some extent Japan; (4) the changing attitudes to Germany, in which, however, an element of fear still exists among the wartime generations. Above all is the conviction that in the long run history is on the side of Russia and the Soviet Union. This conviction is held on nationalistic grounds (that it is now the turn of Russia to enjoy the power and prestige so long denied her), and on ideological grounds (that fundamentally the Soviet system is politically correct, and sooner or later will, through the processes of history, come to be accepted as a model throughout the world). It is, I believe, Brezhnev's and Kosygin's view that, when opportunities present themselves and there is no danger to the security of the Soviet Union, history can, and should, be given a little push in the right direction.

Before leaving the Soviet leadership, we should note one further point. There has been evidence of disagreements within the Soviet leadership, particularly on internal and economic affairs. But, examples of fundamental disagreements on foreign policy and on the view of the balance of power between East and West are hard to come by. We should, therefore, be rather careful about dividing up the present leadership into "hawks" and "doves", that is, two distinct groups led by Brezhnev and Kosygin. Some leaders take hard lines on some subjects, and more moderate lines on others, but the record shows that this leadership has displayed a facility for closing ranks on foreign policy, and the view of their foreign and defense policies offered in this paper is basically supported by a great majority in the Politburo.

SOVIET POLICIES: THE RELATIONSHIP WITH THE UNITED STATES

Now let us look at the priorities to which this group of ambitious, but hardheaded and cautious, men seems to adhere to in pursuing their foreign and defense policies.

There can be no doubt that relations with the United States comes at the head of the list. This is because the Soviet leaders' first care is for the security of the Soviet homeland, and the United States is the only country in the world with greater military strength than the USSR. But, the relationship today goes beyond military factors. Since the Soviet Union achieved superpower status in the late 1960s, two important factors have been introduced into its relationship with the United States. One, the need to prevent the United States from ever moving ahead of the Soviet Union again in terms of strategic power, and two, the need to prevent other powers, e.g. China, Japan, or a future Western Europe, from achieving superpower status. These factors provide much of the rationale of current Soviet policy towards the United States. Put another way, the retention of a "special relationship" with the United States has become a vital interest to the present Soviet leadership. Let us see how this works in practice.

The Soviet Union is basically hostile to the United States. It would like to see a weakening of American power and influence all over the world, primarily in its military support for the West, its military presence in Europe, and the use of its economic power in support of American foreign policy. It would like to see America's alliances disintegrate, and American resolution and determination to aid its friends fade and disappear. But, on certain issues it is equally important to the Russians that the two superpowers should conclude arrangements which cement the Soviet Union's superpower status and make the "special relationship" work. Among the most important of these issues are: (1) the control and limitation of strategic weapons; (2)

Soviet-American trade and exchange of technology; and (3) crisis control. This, to the Russians, means the establishment of procedures and precedents for consultation to prevent the escalation of crises to dangerous proportions. These consultations are also valuable because the Soviet Union, as the newly arrived superpower, is seen by the rest of the world to be treated as an equal by the United States. It is a point of some significance that all three areas in which the Russians want to collaborate with the United States are ones in which they feel actually or potentially weaker than the Americans.

The Soviet leaders are deeply involved in the process of establishing a number of "interlocking" arrangements with the United States in certain specific areas of activity. One of their major fears, as has already been mentioned, is that the United States might want to abandon the "special relationship" in favor of multipolarity: bringing in, or encouraging the acceptance of, China, Japan, or Western Europe, at least as "partial" superpowers. The Soviet leaders are against any such moves because in their view a five-power superpower club would be unstable, and the Soviet Union would be in a permanent minority. Crisis control arrangements would be weakened, and the Soviet Union would no longer enjoy the special relationship which it is now building up with the United States in the fields of strategic weapons limitation, trade, and crisis control policies.

Although the Soviet Union at present places great importance on improving its special relationship with the United States, it also tries to drive the hardest bargain it can with Washington. For example, on SALT II, even after the Vladivostok Accord of November 1974, the Russians held up the negotiations until their new generation of strategic missiles was deployed, so that their most modern weapons would be included in any treaty freezing totals for such strategic weapons. At the same time, the Russians want to insure that the level of strategic armaments agreed to in the SALT talks is high enough numerically, and advanced enough in technology, to deter potential applicants from acquiring this vital attribute of a true superpower. (Large numbers of men, weapons, ships, missiles, and aircraft coincide with traditional Russian concepts of military power.) The Soviet Union i salso seeking most-favored-nation treatment in its trade relationship with the United States, a request which, though favored by the Ford Administration, is opposed by Congress.

On crisis management, the Russians showed, in the various stages of the 1973 Middle East crisis, how anxious they were to appear to be "in on the act" in successful initiatives to control important crises abroad, while avoiding being associated with failures. The same criteria were also applied by the Soviet Union to the Cyprus crisis.

There are two further points which may be relevant to U.S.-Russian relations as seen from Moscow. One is that it would be wrong to give the impression that the Soviet Union is trying to divide up the world with the United States. The fundamental political and economic differences of the United States and the Soviet Union are far too great for that to be part of the Soviet outlook. The other is that nothing in this special relationship with the United States is intended to inhibit the Soviet Union in pursuing its national aims in other confrontations or in other parts of the world. It is to the priorities of these policies that we now turn to in our discussion of Soviet foreign and defense policies.

SOVIET POLICIES TOWARDS EUROPE

When the present Soviet leaders look at their next two priorities, the balance of power in Europe (including the Mediterranean) and the problem of China, it must be hard for them to decide which should come first: China, with its nationalist and ideological hostility to all things Soviet, its great superiority in manpower and its potential nuclear threat to the Soviet Union in the 1980s or later; or Europe, the traditional area of Russian foreign policy where the Soviet leaders seem to believe that their superpower status can help them to shift the European balance of power in their favor. The relationship with China thus seems to be a defensive one, concerned with long term fears; that with Europe has seemed to the present Soviet leaders to contain opportunities for a more active policy in recent years.

Without prejudice to a final judgment on the relative priority of Europe and China to the Soviet leaders, let us look at Europe first. As already mentioned, Europe is the area where Russian foreign policy has always operated (the Russians even had a Mediterranean naval squadron in the 19th century). The Russians feel themselves to be not only the most numerous, but also the greatest of European peoples. They believe, on these grounds and on ideological grounds, that the Soviet Union has the right to greater influence in all European affairs than they have now. Central and Eastern Europe have owed allegiance to the Soviet Union since the War, but the Soviet advancement of her interests further west was halted in 1949. The Russians now feel that the 1949 stalemate is out of date and that they ought to enjoy a balance of power on the Continent more weighted in their favor.

How do the Russians plan to achieve this? Clearly, as long as NATO is effective and the United States guarantee to Western defense is still credible in Moscow, war in Europe is not a feasible method of achieving Soviet aims, which are largely political, though with strategic and economic aspects attached to them. What the Soviet leaders need is a policy which confirms their domination over Eastern Europe (a source of constant anxiety to them, e.g. the 1970 and 1976 riots in Poland and Romania's nagging insubordination) and also gives them some form of constitutional say in the affairs of Western Europe. If some conference or organization could be set up within this framework, the Soviet leaders would hope that by skillful and patient tactics over a long period, they and their successors could begin to influence Western European policies. Even in the short term, an atmosphere might be developed in which NATO would find it difficult to maintain its military strength; differences within the Western Alliance might be exploited, and attempts made to inhibit the nine nations of the EEC from moving forward towards political integration. And, however remote it may seem, let us not lose sight of the kind of Europe which Soviet leaders of the present type would like to see. It is an Eastern Europe firmly under Soviet domination, its political systems and frontiers unchallenged by the West. And, it is a vision of Western Europe divided among itself both politically and economically, without binding military ties or defense links to the United States. Each country would have minimum forces deployed only in its own territory, and would of necessity be persuaded of the need to make its own bilateral deals with the Soviet Union on foreign policy issues.

The principle method chosen by the present Soviet leaders to alter the balance of power in Europe in their favor is negotiation, through the Conference on European Security and Cooperation (CESC). The original Soviet proposal, dating back to 1969, included a draft agenda of three points which explained Soviet intentions very clearly. They were: (1) European and North American acceptance of the postwar frontiers and settlements in Europe, i.e. confirmation of the status quo in Eastern Europe; (2) improved arrangements for trade and technological exchanges; (3) the setting up of an "All European Commission" to discuss European affairs—political, economic, military, and cultural. The Russians also agreed to add another, Western, issue to the agenda: cultural and information exchange involving human contacts. This was an item, however, on which the Russians had serious reservations because of the implications for Communist regimes in Russia and Eastern Europe.

Although the "All-European Commission" was rejected by the Western powers and the neutrals, the Russians still believed that an accord on security and cooperation was worthwhile. The Soviet Union hopes that it will help them to improve their acquisition of Western technology and to exploit opportunities for interfering in the political, economic, and military affairs of Western Europe (for example, the situation in Portugal, Spain, Italy, Greece, or Cyprus).

Similar involvement by the West in East European affairs is ruled out, in the Soviet view, by the agreements on the postwar status quo, as reflected in the first item in the Helsinki Accord. The Russians also want to minimize the effect of the Western clause on human contacts. Although the text of the final Act was not exactly what the Soviet Union wanted, the Soviet leaders still attach great importance to the document because they probably believe that it provides a suitable political framework for their new "activism" in Europe.

One of these new policies associated with this "activism" is called "military détente," which the Russians are now saying should follow the political détente of Helsinki. We can assume that by this is meant a new look at MBFR, on which they hold most of the cards. Their aim is to encourage pressures to build up in Western countries which would favor force reductions in all NATO forces (especially the Bundeswehr), withdrawals of troops (particularly American forces back to the United States), limitations on reinforcements into the European area, and cuts in defense expenditures. The Soviet Union would then adjust the military balance in Europe at a new lower level of forces which would still give the Warsaw Pact an increased relative advantage over NATO in Central Europe. In the meantime, as a characteristic measure of military reinsurance, the Soviet Union continues to improve its forces in Eastern Europe, both in numbers and quality, and to call for a strengthening of the Warsaw Pact. Indeed, one of the strongest supports of the Soviet position in Europe is the great strength and diversity of its armies, navies, and air forces, backed by the strategic nuclear arsenal which has done so much to win superpower status for the Soviet Union.

In present circumstances the Soviet leaders feel no significant economic constraints on the stationing of conventional forces in Eastern Europe at their present levels, nor do they have to contend with a parliament or public opinion critical of defense or military expenditure. Therefore, whatever the outcome of talks on force reductions may be, we may be sure that the Soviet Union will continue to strengthen its forces in the European area qualitatively on land, sea, and in the air, as a general background to its political attempt to shift the balance of power in Europe to its advantage. But, it is possible that in order to keep the initiative on MBFR in Soviet hands now that the

CSCE is over, the Soviet Union may offer new proposals on MBFR. This could take the form of a new draft treaty or greater readiness to consider existing Western proposals more seriously.

THE SOVIET UNION AND CHINA

Some doubt was expressed earlier as to which of the Soviet Union's preoccupations, Europe or China, had priority in Soviet eyes in the present phase of Soviet thinking on the balance of power. Certainly the problem of China raises some very basic issues for the Soviet leaders. They cannot ignore a 4,000-mile-long disputed frontier and many historical and nationalist issues between them, some with racialist overtones. Soviet fears of China's numerical superiority, future nuclear potential, and ideological claims to be the true interpreters of the Communist belief have already been mentioned. To these fundamental anxieties have been added the effects of China's emergence some years ago from the Cultural Revolution into "diplomatic respectability." China's use of her membership in the Security Council in the United Nations to propagate her anti-Soviet thesis, her mending of fences with many countries of the Western world, her approving comments on the EEC and NATO, and her campaign to advance Chinese interests in the Third World to the detriment of the Soviet Union's effort there all contribute to these anxieties.

The Russians are especially dismayed and worried about the new, if tenuous, contacts between China and the United States and Japan. The Russians do not, of course, exaggerate the extent of these contacts, or their potential, and they are fairly realistic on likely limitations to their further development. But the mere fact that they have taken place and are still continuing is worrysome, and the Soviet Union is especially concerned at the prospect of Japan and China getting together; hence their anxiety over the Sino-Japanese Treaty negotiations with its reference to the "hegemony" clause. While the full effects of this situation may be seen only in the future, the Soviet Union already feels the "odd man out" in the East Asian "Quadrilateral": the United States, China, Japan, and Russia. The U.S.-USSR "special relationship" does not appear to extend to the local power balance in the Far East. The Soviet Union is reluctant to satisfy Japanese territorial demands (the cession of a number of small islands in the Soviet-held Kurile chain of islands), and Soviet economic blandishments to Japan to encourage her to participate in the economic exploitation of Siberia do not yet seem to be cast in terms acceptable to the Japanese government or the business community (who would have to provide the necessary finance). Negotiations on this aspect, however, do continue between the two countries.

What then, can the Soviet Union do about its confrontation with China? Politically very little, except to keep its concept of an Asian security organization alive (a proposal which has been resurrected in the wake of the CSCE and the fall of Vietnam and Cambodia), strengthen its ties with India (the other power which fears Chinese influence in Asia), counter Chinese activities in the Third World, and await developments in the post-Mao era. The Soviet government will then assess the attitudes and policies of Mao's successors to see if there is any possibility that they might retreat from some of Mao's more extreme anti-Soviet policies, perhaps for economic or technological reasons.

There seems to be no logical case for a Soviet military attack on China. though the Chinese seem to fear one. No one in Moscow could either guarantee the outcome of such a conflict, even of a so-called "surgical strike" against Chinese nuclear plants or bases, or contemplate either the nuclear destruction or conventional conquest of China. But the Russians will continue to retain as a garrison very large ground, sea, and air forces in the border area of the Far East. These now amount to about forty-five divisions and 1,200 aircraft. They are deployed to deal with any emergencies and to insure that any future discussions with China will be held from a position of strength.

SOVIET POLICIES BEYOND THE BALANCE OF POWER

So far we have discussed the three major elements in the Soviet Union's foreign and defense policy: relationships with the United States, Europe, and China. In many ways, however, Soviet activity in other parts of the world has become more dramatic and, on the surface at least, more characteristic of a newly arrived superpower anxious to flex its muscles and experiment with its ability to expand its influence in areas of the world further away from the Soviet homeland (especially where Western withdrawals appear to have left power vacuums).

The Soviet Union is convinced that a superpower should have the right to extend its influence to various parts of the world, using, in particular, its naval and air power, its economic wealth (through military and economic aid programs), propaganda, subversion (where appropriate), and other political means. In doing so the Soviet Union hopes to weaken Western and Chinese influence and inhibit the freedom of action of its rivals and opponents, often on a largely opportunistic basis. Indeed, the Soviet Union has now considerable experience in operating naval and air forces in distant waters and unfamiliar surroundings. It has administered economic and military aid programs in counties as far apart as Angola, Cuba and Vietnam. It is beginning to learn something of the difficulties in acquiring what it really wants—reliable political influence (which it could use for strategic purposes if necessary)—in non-Communist countries far from the land frontier of the Soviet Union. Nevertheless, for these superpower reasons, and because the present Soviet leaders still feel a sense of political mission in formulating their foreign policies, the Soviet Union intends to continue following active policies abroad. It hopes to weaken and undermine the influence of the West and China, and increase Soviet influence wherever possible, on a largely opportunistic basis.

Within this framework, there are a number of areas in which the Russians are principally engaged. They include the Middle East, South Asia, the Indian Ocean, and the Caribbean. The Middle East is complicated by the fact that it is so close to the area of Soviet confrontation with NATO in the Mediterranean that it is sometimes hard to distinguish Soviet measures relating to NATO from politico-military activity in the Middle East proper. For example, the independent Soviet naval air presence which was established in Egypt until July 1972 was used simply as a counter to NATO and had little to do with the defense of Egypt.

Soviet policies in the Middle East are also complicated by the oil factors. The Russians appreciate the reliance of Western countries and Japan on Middle East oil supplies and the potential vulnerability of oil supply routes to these countries. Hence they do play a role in Middle East oil politics (notably in Iraq). On the whole, however, the Russians' behavior so far suggests that they are hesitant about entering the field of international oil politics in support of their foreign policies, because of the complexity of the factors and the worldwide interests of the many nations, companies, and institutions involved. The present Soviet leaders probably think that their best policy is to encourage the oil producing countries to nationalize the oil industries, to increase their participation in them, and to raise prices for Western customers.

Looking at Soviet policy towards the Middle East as a whole, the major Soviet effort to gain influence goes into economic and military aid, especially in key countries like Syria, Iraq, South Yemen, Libya, Somalia, and Egypt (although Egypt has recently more or less slipped out of the Soviet military aid network). Current Soviet tactics also involve an increase in contacts between the Soviet Communist Party and the political elites which rule these countries. This is done in the hope of building up groups of pro-Soviet politicians or soldiers who will eventually come to power. Of course, the Russians experience setbacks, such as that suffered when Egypt expelled the Soviet military presence in 1972, an act which probably taught the Soviet Union a lesson in the doubtful value of military installations abroad as a basis of political influence. Syria, which receives large amounts of Soviet weapons, may have been under some kind of Soviet pressure to allow the establishment of alternative Soviet military facilities, but so far has not placed herself in the position Egypt was before July 1972. On the other hand, Iraq and South Yemen have been moving in the opposite direction. Iraq signed a treaty with the Soviet Union in 1972, and the Iraqis have turned to the Russians for help in dealing with their newly-nationalized oil fields and even in internal political matters. The Soviet Union has had some success recently in combating Chinese influence in South Yemen, to which the Russians supplied an air force in 1973, and in increasing Soviet influence in Aden in the political and military fronts.

Since the October 1973 War, the Soviet Union has followed an opportunistic, yet cautious policy in the Middle East. Basically what the Soviet Union wants out of the present situation in the Middle East is a return to a new version of the no-peace, no-war position more political influence in Cairo and Damascus, a capability to exploit the reopening of the Suez Canal for commercial and strategic reasons, and a reversal of the current trend toward improved Egyptian-Western relations, which the Russians bitterly resent, though they seem to see little hope of doing this while President Sadat is in power in Cairo.

The Soviet Union is also increasing its interest in India. Here the Soviet motive is to obtain political influence in the second largest country in Asia as a counterweight to China. (India is also the most important country of the Indian Ocean area, and is now a nuclear power.) The Soviet Union was originally able to gain prestige and some influence in India through its support for the Indian cause in the war with Pakistan, and has tried to develop this influence further in the present internal political situation in India. The Soviet Union maintains a naval squadron permanently based in the Indian Ocean, and is acquiring shore facilities for this squadron in at least one of the littoral countries, Somalia. It seems likely that the Soviet Union wants to use its naval presence in support of the general task of limiting Western options in the Indian Ocean, conducting surveillance of Diego Garcia, combating Chinese and Western influence in littoral countries, and increasing Soviet influence, especially in the area bordering on the Middle East.

Looking further East, the Soviet Union has long been involved in Indo-China, and since the fall of South Vietnam and Cambodia to the Communists, has been engaged in a struggle to combat Chinese influence in this area as a whole. In this struggle, in which both Communist leaderships have to contend with the very tough and confident North Vietnamese, the Chinese have the advantage of proximity, and greater influence in Cambodia. The Russians have the advantage of a better position in Vietnam, partly because of the quality of the aid they can offer in the vital tasks of reconstruction. But both will struggle hard to secure political primacy in Indochina to the exclusion of the other, and thus improve the balance of power in Southeast Asia in its favor.

The Soviet Union does not yet regard Latin America and the Caribbean as affecting the balance of power. It will base its policies on the exploitation of the political situation as it develops, on a largely opportunistic basis. They have for example used Conakry in Guinea as a base for long-range reconnaissance flights over the Atlantic. They will watch the situation closely for useful opportunities, continue to supply economic and military aid, and challenge Western and Chinese influence. Angola is one of the countries where such a policy has crystallized. They will also continue to support their Caribbean outpost, Cuba, economically and with military aid, perhaps hoping, in a very discreet fashion, to increase its usefulness to Soviet naval deployments without unduly antagonizing the United States.

It has been possible to treat only these interesting, and in some cases dramatic, examples of Soviet world wide policies rather briefly, perhaps even superficially. Each of them, of course, has its intrinsic importance and value for the Soviet Union, but this point illustrates the real nature of Soviet foreign and defense policies. The Soviet Union's main preoccupations are with its national security, its superpower status, its relationship with the United States, its confrontation with the West in Europe, and its problems with China. In some senses, the Middle East is near enough to one of those areas (Europe and the Mediterranean) to be partially involved in those fundamental relationships, and Japan is an essential element in the balance of power in the Far East. Activity in the rest of the world is regarded in Moscow as a vital aspect of a superpower's rights and duties. But, it is still very much as a "bonus" in Soviet foreign policies, and the effect on the balance of power is not yet really significant. This could change, possibly under a new Soviet leadership. New setbacks could cause a slackening of activity in certain parts of the world, new successes could lead to a strengthening of Soviet interests in some of these areas of operation.

We cannot, therefore, predict how this aspect of Soviet policies will develop, but we can offer one or two conclusions. The first is that now that the Soviet Union has achieved superpower status, it still has to work very hard in order to retain its political and military "parity" with the United States. It will not give up its drive to do this, in spite of the adverse consequences to the Soviet economy which the effort involves. The second is that if the present outlook in Moscow prevails, we in the West are likely to face a great deal of political and politico-military activism on the part of the Soviet Union. However, the new Soviet activism will be tempered by internal political developments in the Soviet leadership, the Soviet-U.S. relationship, the Soviet economy, and the longer term effect of China's growth towards superpower status. It will be tempered above all by the Soviet conviction that policies which could lead to a military clash with the United States and NATO cannot be feasible ones for the achievement of Soviet foreign policy goals.

Europe's Economic Vulnerability and Political Weakness: Implications for the West

Andrew J. Pierre

Western Europe became more economically vulnerable and politically unstable in 1974-75 than at any time since the early postwar years. In a wider sense, the European condition was part of the newly perceived "crisis" in the West, or, what the Soviets have been calling the "crisis of capitalism." Although the crisis had major economic components, it was equally significant because of its political dimensions, many of which were induced by economic factors, but others, such as the revolution in Portugal, had occurred for non-economic reasons. Altogether Western Europe entered into a period of extraordinary flux and transition. Within less than two years, fourteen of NATO's fifteen nations changed governments. Events in the Eastern Mediterranean, especially the clash of the Greeks and Turks on Cyprus, combined with changes in the Western Mediterranean, notably the revolution in Portugal and the commencement of an overdue transition in Spain, raised new questions about the durability of the NATO alliance. An unusually deep political uncertainty clouded the future in some of Europe's major powers, particularly in Great Britain and Italy, and the future of the European Economic Community (EEC) came into greater doubt than ever. The economic crisis, as manifested by inflation, recession, and unemployment, fostered social tensions within national societies. Differing rates of inflation, and monetary policies that varied from country to country, created additional stress within the EEC. For all these reasons a new, pervasive sense of vulnerability and malaise seized Western Europe. It could not help but have an important impact upon the European-American relationship.

Unlike the early postwar years, when the danger to Western societies was clear and present, today's challenges are not clear-cut, and the solutions are hardly self-evident. Then, a security threat to Western Europe led to the creation of NATO, and the need for postwar reconstruction led to the Marshall Plan. The causes of today's problems are more difficult to assess. Recession, spiraling inflation, an uncertain energy "crisis", and the unprecedented transfer of resources to the oil producing countries are complex and interrelated phenomena with no easy answers. Reasonable men differ in both their analysis and the proposed remedies. To this must be added attitudinal differences between the older and younger generations, as well as shifting ideological alignments within societies. The new economic stress and social tensions are creators of political instability. Yet what is at stake is remarkably similar to the situation of thirty years ago—in fundamental terms it is no less than the maintenance of free and democratic societies.

The Yom Kippur War and the related events beginning in the fall of 1973 are clearly a watershed in the evolution of the postwar world. The oil embargo and the consequent quintupling of the price of petroleum led to a disequilibration of the world economic system from which we have yet to fully recover. And, whatever will be the new equilibrium in the terms of trade and the balance of payments, it will differ significantly from the earliest era. Yet, it is important to recall that today's problems are of longer term origin. The international monetary system was shaken by successive devaluations, and the action undertaken unilaterally by the United States on 15 August 1971. The sudden transition from fixed to floating exchange rates, and the somewhat chauvinistic approach of Secretary of the Treasury John Connally, tended to disrupt the cooperative pattern of international management of the noncommunist economic system. Already in the late 1960s there were serious differences on trade issues between Europe and America which contributed to the difficulty in commencing the General Agreement on Tariffs and Trade (GATT) negotiations. The EEC was making only limited progress towards the goals set for 1980 in the Werner Report on monetary integration and a more advanced customs union. The question of the maintenance of U.S. troops in Europe was under intense debate in the early 1970s with the near passage of the Mansfield Resolution. Finally, the Year of Europe exercise, begun with Henry Kissinger's speech of April 1973, had an extremely divisive effect within the Alliance. Foreign offices found themselves needlessly entangled with the wording of declarations intended to codify the European-American relationship. West European states resisted the linkage of economic with security issues, suspecting that this would lead to a form of subtle blackmail because of Europe's continuing dependency upon American protection for its security. The United States appeared to resist the development of a European political identity and was felt to be showing a loss of interest in the goals of European unity. With these trends providing the background in the fall of 1973, the ensuing crisis was, to a now often forgotten extent, the magnification of an existing and developing situation.

Europe's vulnerability is as much political and psychological as it is economic. Indeed, in the economic area the dislocations thus far have not been as great as were once expected and feared. As any traveler within Europe can attest, there has been little evidence of an energy shortage. Even during the oil embargo some shipments of oil managed to reach European ports. The drain on the nations' balance of payments as a consequence of the rise in the price of oil, though considerable, has been far less than was once feared. This is particularly evident in Italy, which once was headed towards national bankruptcy but which by the summer of 1975 was able to finance oil imports far better than expected. By mid-1975, estimates of the projected balance of payments outflows to the oil producing countries for the remainder of the decade were within manageable proportions. This rosy picture can, of course, change within a short time period. A severe winter could greatly increase the demand of oil for heating. A return to economic prosperity could, paradoxically, have some undesirable effects if the increase in foreign exchange earnings due to exports does not offset the increase in the consumption and price of oil. More importantly, a renewed oil embargo as a consequence of another Arab-Israeli war, coupled with another major increase in the price of oil, could have disastrous economic consequences for Western Europe.

Nevertheless, it is Europe's political vulnerability which may, in the long term, be the most significant. This political softness suddenly became very apparent as a result of the oil embargo. Rather than acting in concert, each country went off on its own pursuing a highly nationalistic and independent policy. Thus there was little in the way of a common European policy towards the Arab countries, nor did the energy crisis stimulate a common energy policy for the EEC countries. Nations made their separate long-term deals with individual OPEC exporters in order to assure their own availability of supply. This tendency could not help but have a deleterious impact upon Brussels and the development of the European Community. Progress in the construction of Community institutions, and in the development of its political identity, came to a virtual halt. The task of statesmen during the past two years has been less that of political construction than the avoidance of serious political erosion. If the Community was analogous to a house in construction, awaiting its completion with the placement of a roof (in the form of direct elections to a European Parliament and greater supranational power for the commissioners of the EEC), it now had to keep the four walls from tumbling down. This was most apparent in the difficulty in dealing with problems internal to the Community, such as the differing rates of inflation and their impact on exchange rates, but it was also evident in the Community's political dialogue with the external world where the attempt to unite, so as to speak to the United States with a single voice, was virtually dropped. The fledgling movement towards consultations and cooperative arrangements on defense was also abandoned.

More important still than the erosion of the European Community was the increasing political instability in the southern tier of Europe, namely in Italy, Portugal, Spain, Greece, and Turkey. Generalizations about these countries tend to break down when subjected to close scrutiny. Although these countries have some points in common, the observer is more impressed by the distinctly national character of the political dynamics in each one. Nevertheless, for the outside world the significant perspective was the new condition of transition in Southern Europe and its prospective impact on the organizational institutions of NATO and the EEC.

Italy is the country which should be of the greatest concern, although it is Portugal which has received the most attention. Italy is geographically located in the heart of Europe and in the center of the Mediterranean. A dramatic change in Italy would disrupt both NATO and the EEC, whereas the ongoing transition in Portugal can be relatively contained. A "Communist" Italy would have greater long-term impact than a "Communist" Portugal. Italy moves from crisis to crisis and it is difficult at any given moment to make a confident judgment regarding the seriousness of its condition. In 1974 Italy had the highest rate of inflation in Western Europe at 25 percent, the worst unemployment situation on the continent, and the biggest balance of payments deficit. It was hardest hit by the oil crisis, with the oil deficit alone amounting to $10 billion. A $2 billion grant from the Federal Republic of Germany in August 1974 was essential to Italy's continuing solvency. Out of this dire situation, and to the surprise of many, Italy made a considerable recovery during 1975 and substantially improved its trade balance. Although the Italian economy may continue to improve, there is no assurance of this given its structural defects, and the long-term economic situation remains uncertain.

Italy has been paying a substantial political price for its economic condition. A persistent problem of unemployment and a high level of inflation have led to a considerable amount of social discontent and unrest, which is afflicting large portions of Italian society. Recent years have seen a great increase in terrorist incidents, violence, and in the kidnapping of prominent or wealthy individuals. There has been a marked polarization of Italian society with the growth of extremist groups on both the Left and the Right. Continuing strikes have disabled large sectors of industry. Outside observers have come to question the long-term stability of Italy, given that the glue that has successfully held Italian society together in the past seems to be melting away.

A coalition government including the participation of the Communist Party now appears quite possible—to some inevitable—within this decade. The only alternative may be an early revitalization of the Christian Democratic Party, but whether it is capable of this given its complacency and political sclerosis is doubtful. Indeed, much of Italy is already run with Communist participation, as they constitute the largest party in the biggest cities: Rome, Bologna, Milan, Naples, Turin, Genoa, and Florence. As many as six of the country's twenty regions now have Communist governments. The historical compromise, or "compromesso storico," suggested by the head of the Italian Communist Party, Enrico Berlinguer, has support within elements of the Christian Democratic Party, the Republican Party, and the Socialist Parties. Other members of these parties remain strongly opposed to a historical compromise, but it is uncertain how long they will be able to hold out. In the regional and local elections of June 1975, with the 18-21 year-olds voting for the first time, the Italian Communist Party made strong gains. They received 32.4 percent of the vote in comparison to 27.5 percent in 1972, and the Socialist Party also made a significant advance. The political import of a coalition government would depend greatly upon the nature of the coalition and the policies it pursues, but, inevitably, as will be discussed, the implications for NATO and Europe would be considerable.

The situation in Portugal is quite different from that of Italy, and is in no real way related, in its origins, to the economic and energy crisis. The coup carried out in Lisbon on 25 April 1974 by the young officers of the Armed Forces Movement marked the end of forty-eight years of authoritarian rule under the conservative regime of Salazar, and that of his more pragmatic successor Marcello Caetano. The former regime's hardline commitment to retaining Portugal's overseas possessions, and its inability to foster the social and economic development of Portugal, caused the country to fall behind the more highly industrialized European states. The coup was the result of the developing view that the conflicts in the African territories either could not be won or were too costly, with nearly half of the national budget going into military expenditures, thereby taking up resources which might otherwise have contributed to the development of the economy. It brought into the open the formerly clandestine Communist and Socialist parties, which showed remarkable organization once they were able to surface. The Communist Party, especially under the leadership of dogmatic Alvaro Cunhal, has shown a strong discipline among its hard core membership, as well as an allegiance to an outmoded Stalinist ideology. Although the junior ranking officers who captured the leadership of the Armed Forces Movement are only partially Communist, with many other officers more sympathetic to the Socialist or Republican parties, the Communists for a time managed to penetrate Portuguese institutions in a way out of proportion to their numbers. The true political inclination of Portuguese society as a whole was vividly demonstrated in the national election to a Constituent Assembly held on 25 April 1975, on the first anniversary of the coup. To the surprise of most observers abroad, the Communist Party received only a very low vote, 12-13 percent, in the context of a very high electoral turnout. The massive support given to the non-Communist Left, particularly the Socialist Party under the leadership of Mario Soares, was the best possible indication of the wishes of the Portuguese people. Nevertheless, the Communists remain an important political factor as the other parties were forced, prior to the vote, to agree that the military would remain in power for several more years on the fallacious assumption that the country, having just emerged from half a century of nondemocratic rule, was not prepared for an open parliamentary system with the normal play of political parties.

Developments in Portugal are of concern to the Western Alliance for a number of reasons. As a member of NATO, Portugal is the first alliance member which has threatened to become a Communist state, thus creating serious political and organizational problems for the military structure. If, as has been reported, the Soviet Union is interested in acquiring naval bases along the Atlantic shore of Portugal, this could pose a problem for the maintenance of Atlantic sea lanes. The Azores base is of considerable importance to the United States in case of the need for American reinforcements in a war in the Middle East or in Europe. The new Portuguese government has indicated that it would not make the base available in case of a renewed Arab-Israeli conflict, and it is conceivable that the same would apply to a conflict in Europe should Portugal become a neutral state. Moreover, what is at stake in Portugal, as the struggle continues for its future political direction, is of considerable consequence to the other Socialist parties of Western Europe. If the non-Communist Left in Portugal, despite its overwhelming support among the population, is not able to prevent a total takeover by a Communist Party giving its allegiance to the Soviet Union, the lesson which will be drawn in other countries such as France and Italy is that a Socialist-Communist alliance (which came extremely close to electing François Mitterrand in France in 1974) cannot be trusted to maintain its independence and prevent a Communist takeover.

The coming political evolution in Spain is another factor of great uncertainty, but one of enormous consequence for Western Europe as a whole. Spain is a country of 36 million which since 1959 has undergone impressive economic growth. It has also lived under almost four decades of authoritarian rule and political repression. In recent years there has been a tendency towards the polarization of political groupings in anticipation of the post-Franco era. The task of the new king, Carlos I, will be to choose a degree and pace of liberalization which will avoid open conflict between the well entrenched Falangists on the Right and those on the Left who wish to see Spain adopt democratic institutions similar to those existing in the rest of Western Europe. A reform of the political system which avoids a clash between opposing elements of Spanish society will be no easy task, but the alternative of a degeneration into a new and dreadful civil war cannot be totally ruled out. A complicating factor is the existence of extremist and separatist groups, such as the Basque ETA terrorist organization, who may not be willing to work within the new political framework, even if it leads towards a democratic, multiparty political system.

Spain will present a challenge to Western Europe because of its likely desire in the coming period to enter the European Economic Community (EEC) and NATO. Thoughtful Spaniards recognize the importance of such steps for the economic and political well-being of their country, and will use this as an argument in favor of internal reform. Europeans will have to recognize that they can no longer exclude Spain on the basis of ideological and political objections to the Franco regime. It will be necessary, therefore, to make judgments regarding the gradual liberalization of Spanish society, bearing in mind the risk of the Communist Party becoming an important actor in this large, populous, and strategically important country. Should Spain be accepted into the EEC it would also be desirable to bring it into NATO, so as to secure the availability of the American air and naval bases.

At the other end of the Mediterranean, Greece and Turkey have weakened the Western position as the consequence of their struggle over Cyprus. The Greek attempt to replace Archbishop Makarios with the unsavory Nikas Sampson, and the subsequent Turkish invasion of Cyprus, which the U.S. was either unable or unwilling, through its diplomacy, to avoid (in contrast to the successful intervention of Cyrus Vance in 1967 which prevented a similar invasion) has placed two NATO partners at loggerheads. The possibility of renewed fighting is ever present despite the on-again-off-again negotiations. Meanwhile, Greece has moved out of the military organization of NATO, although in fact the withdrawal was only partially implemented with Greek officers remaining attached to the various NATO commands. Because of the decision of the U.S. Congress to cut off arms aid to Turkey as a consequence of its invasion of Cyprus, Ankara closed U.S. bases in Turkey. Although the ban on arms has now been lifted, Turkish-American relations remain delicate, and lack of progress in the negotiations on Cyprus could lead to a restoration of the arms ban. The same thing is occurring with U.S. bases in Greece, where home-porting arrangements for U.S. aircraft carriers of the Sixth Fleet are to be terminated, and some U.S. bases are being closed. And yet another dispute between Greece and Turkey has arisen out of their respective claims over oil drilling rights in the Aegean Sea, where considerable deposits of oil and natural gas have been reported around Greek-owned islands close to the Turkish coast.

The net result of all these events is that the attention of Ankara and Athens has been turned from their common security concerns regarding any potential threat from the East towards the dispute between each other. In the process, the United States has been denounced by the Greeks for supporting Turkey, and by the Turks for cutting off arms aid to them. As long as these nations remain close to the brink of war, the Eastern Mediterranean will remain a vulnerable area in the overall East-West balance.

What has been the impact of the economic crisis and the ongoing political change in Southern Europe upon the Atlantic Alliance, and what can we expect in the future? Clearly there has been some erosion of defense efforts as a consequence of economic difficulties, as seen in the reduced defense budgets in Britain, the Netherlands, and Denmark. But, contrary to the popular impression, it has been less than one might expect. Altogether, NATO-wide defense expenditures have remained fairly stable at about 4 percent of GNP for the past five years. The defense cutbacks of Britain have been limited to reductions outside of Europe. In Germany and in France, military expenditures have remained about level, and in the United States, projected spending was increased, with the "turn around" defense budget for fiscal year 1975-76. Two new brigades are to be assigned to the U.S. Seventh Army in Germany, and one is to be stationed along the North German Plain, which has always been considered a weak point because of its vulnerability as the most likely spot for an invasion. Congress has rejected efforts to decrease the U.S. military establishment, and, in the wake of the end of the war in Vietnam, agreed to augment the number of U.S. combat divisions from thirteen to sixteen.

There has been a weakening of the alliance's base structure, as indicated above, but this is due more to political factors essentially unrelated to the economic crisis than to anything else. Planners must assume that the Azores base will not be available now in case of a war in the Middle East, but a growing political movement on the Azores islands, which supports the retention of U.S. bases and disassociates itself from the leftist elements in Portugal, puts some constraints upon the ability of Lisbon to exclude the United States altogether. Even though Greece has partially withdrawn from the military organization of the alliance, some U.S. bases are being maintained, particularly the strategically located air base in Crete. Although some of the twenty U.S. bases in Turkey will no doubt remain closed, it is unlikely that the United States will be forced to withdraw completely. The fact is that in neither Athens nor Ankara is there any inclination to withdraw from NATO, since political leaders in these two countries continue to attach the highest priority to the retention of the links with Western Europe and the United States which the alliance provides.

Given an increasingly uncertain future, it does not require an extraordinary leap of the imagination to assume a situation in which Italy had a coalition government with Communist participation, and Portugal, in one form or another, also had a Communist-oriented government. This would clearly alter NATO in a radical manner and require some change in its political structure. There would be an increasing concentration upon the center of Europe, in particular the Federal Republic of Germany, Belgium, and Holland. Even with the assumption that France would not return to the military organization of the alliance, its geographical location would give it increasing importance.

Much would depend, however, upon the nature of the Communist participation in government. One would have to make a careful country-by-country analysis in order to come to a measured judgment concerning what the response of democratic governments should be. Among the questions one would want answered are: What is the nature of the Communist participation and which ministries are in fact controlled by Communist ministers? How strong are the other parties in a coalition? What is the attitude of the Communists toward NATO and the United States? What is their attitude towards the Soviet Union? Who controls the army and the internal security forces? What types of political alignments and stresses exist within the Communist Party of the country involved? What are the generational and other differences in attitudes of the Party leaders and of their followers? And, most importantly in those cases where the Communists only have a partial access to power, will they be satisfied with some participation in power or will they seek full control of the country?

The complexities implicit in the above questions suggest the need for a very sophisticated and carefully developed policy of what should be the attitude of the United States and the remaining NATO countries towards coalition governments which include Communist ministers. It would be a mistake to assume, as was once done at the highest level in Washington, that NATO could not live with "partial membership" or "special arrangements." This has already been the case with regard to France, and more recently Greece. There is no reason why it cannot be accepted in other countries should it prove to be regrettably but unavoidably necessary. Nor should the Western countries fall into the trap of saying, as in the case of Portugal, that governments with Communist participation cannot, *a priori*, remain in NATO. This is too simplistic an approach and could, indeed, prove to be self-defeating. Some adjustments would be required, such as the withdrawal of such countries from the Nuclear Planning Group of NATO, and NATO would no doubt become a different type of political organization. But to rule out the participation of governments which include Communist ministers might result in forcing them more and more into becoming full Communist satellite states under the direction of the Soviet Union. A wiser policy might be to give full assistance to those elements, including Socialist parties, which are in coalition with Communist parties, but which are attempting to resist the drawing of their countries into the Soviet orbit. In other words, rather than shaking the big stick, we might consider assisting the non-Communist Left and seek access to it in order to have influence upon it.

Looking at the trans-Atlantic relationship, we can see that the impact of the economic and political crisis has been to strengthen the comparative weight of the United States in the European-American balance. This has not been the result of an alleged attempt to restore American "hegemony," whatever that means, nor has it been the intentional aim of U.S. policy. Rather, it has been an unavoidable consequence of the newly perceived Western European vulnerability. Today the economic clashes of the late 1960s and early 1970s, the verbal gymnastics of the "Year of Europe," and the Jobert-Kissinger dueling over the leadership of Europe, all seem very much like ancient history. We are much more aware of comparative American strengths and European weaknesses. The United States is less reliant than Western Europe upon imported raw materials and is also less dependent upon foreign trade. Unlike Europe, the United States is a net supplier of food, and it is the main provider of the increasingly important commodity of enriched uranium. The dollar remains the accepted international standard, especially with the weakening of the pound. American industry has proven to be more attractive to Arab investors than that of Western Europe. Factors such as these, and others, have combined to make the United States much more independent, and give it a far greater freedom of maneuverability than the Western European states.

Moreover, many of the emerging global problems are ones which cannot be handled separately by Western Europe without the United States. This has become especially clear in the light of the energy crisis. The creation of the International Energy Agency within the Organization of Economic Co-operation and Development (OECD) for the purpose of managing the energy resources of the consumer countries and carrying on the dialogue with the producers, as well as the Kissinger-Simon plan for a $25 billion financial safety net to deal with the problem of recycling, are not, as seen by some, deliberate attempts to reassert American dominance and leadership. Rather, they are manifestations of the fact that many problems can only be dealt with in a broader political fremework. This applies not only to energy, but also to other areas in the management of the world's resources such as food, raw materials, and the environment.

Another reason for the relative improvement in Atlantic relations has been the end of the Vietnam war. Most Western Europeans did not support the United States in this venture beyond the late 1960s and tended to question American wisdom and political maturity. Despite the unfortunate manner in which the war came to its final close, most West Europeans are now heartened that the war is totally over. For a while there was a tendency on the part of some Europeans to draw rather sweeping generalizations, and to see a worldwide erosion of U.S. commitments and a drift to isolationism. Looked at in terms of American interests, however, there was never any real comparison between Vietnam and Western Europe. The American commitment in Vietnam never had as much public support in the United States as our commitment to Western Europe. To many, the loss of South Vietnam had been expected as far back as the Tet offensive, or the decision of President Johnson not to run for reelection, or, in some cases, the final pullout of U.S. combat troops after the Paris accords. All that was not predictable was its final timing and the pace and manner of the end of the war. In the post-Vietnam period there will be a reappraisal of U.S. foreign commitments. This will concentrate on Asia, in particularly Korea, Japan, Thailand, and perhaps the Philippines. In the total context of U.S. foreign policy, however, the result of the loss of Vietnam will be to give still greater priority to the American commitment in Europe. Unlike Asia, Western Europe remains truly vital—indeed the *most* vital overseas interest of the United States. Americans understand that the Soviet-American political balance runs through Europe, and that America's own security depends upon the security of Europe. The economic investment on the continent has no comparison elsewhere, and, finally, the close ties of history, blood, and culture, are, in the last analysis, so great that no monetary or other appraisal can accord them their proper value.

For the Soviet Union the political consequences of the economic crisis in the Western world have posed particular dilemmas. Ostensibly the "general crisis of capitalism" has provided the Soviet Union with an unrivaled opportunity to press forward against the West, taking advantage of its economic disarray. Analysis of the nature of the economic crisis made in the Soviet Union have noted the unprecedented combination of inflation, unemployment, and raw material shortages in a large number of the major capitalist countries. Along with these economic factors has occurred the sudden acceleration of political change in Portugal, the new situation in post-Franco Spain, and the difficulties for the West created by the conflict in Cyprus.

Despite what might be perceived as novel and immense opportunities for the advancement of Soviet interests in Western Europe, actual Soviet policy has been marked by considerable moderation and restraint. In Italy the Communist Party has not been encouraged to press now for a historical compromise leading to participation in the government. In France, the Soviet ambassador to Paris made an intervention in the closing stages of the Presidential election in support of Giscard d'Estaing, thus indicating to many voters that Moscow did not wish to see the Communist Party come into power at this time. Although the Soviet Union has given assistance to the Communist Party in Portugal, the extent of that assistance remains somewhat uncertain and is clearly less than what might be possible.

Soviet leaders, in their statements and in their writings, appear somewhat perplexed by the nature and depth of the economic crisis in the West. They are not certain whether it represents a basic, fundamental crisis which will produce important changes in the existing political and economic structure of the West or whether it is of a more transitionary nature, unlikely to have long-term consequences. Such confusion and puzzlement are, of course, also to be found within our own analysis in the West. But for Soviet leaders it presents particular dilemmas concerning the opportunities which they should seize or pass up. The failure in resolving these dilemmas has led to a somewhat ambivalent policy.

Nevertheless, one can identify a number of sound reasons for the relative restraint in Soviet policy. First, Moscow places considerable value upon the eonomic assistance and technical exchange which it receives as a consequence of good relations with Western Europe. Trade with France, Britain and the Federal Republic of Germany is assisted by credits from these countries, and an aggressive Soviet policy towards Western Europe would no doubt dampen, if not totally impede, the further development of trade. Second, Brezhnev is committed to the success of his détente policy. More specifically, this has required all his political ability to present to the 25th Party Congress such agreements as the CSCE Protocol in a positive light even though they have suffered considerably from a deterioration of East-West relations. Third, the Soviets seem constrained to have been sobered by the lesson of Chile, learning that a trend towards the left can lead to a Rightist or "fascist" backlash or takeover. This is the danger in both Italy and Portugal. They are aware that serious economic instability can undermine the position of the Left and lead to a turn towards the extreme Right. Accordingly, the Soviet Union has contented itself with maintaining the status quo in France and Italy, and has given only limited support to its followers in Portugal. Fourth, taking advantage of West European weakness might have the effect of helping pull Western Europe together. From the perspective of the Soviet Union, a Western Europe which remains vulnerable and lacking in confidence is more attractive than one which, fearful of the Soviet Union, decides to increase its defense efforts. Indirectly the Soviet Union profits from West European weakness as it is able to get more trade on better terms because of the West European need to control recession and inflation through expansion of industry and exports.

These reasons for the Soviet's relative restraint cannot assure the West, however, that Moscow's moderation and ambivalence will continue. Changes within the Soviet Union, and increased or different opportunities, may lead to another set of policy conclusions. We know that within the Politburo, there are those who would give far less priority to the maintenance of détente, and, who would prefer a more activist Soviet foreign policy combined with a greater degree of self-dependence in the economic sphere. Given the pattern of change in the political leadership in that country, we can have little assurance that less moderate leaders may not come into prominence. The changing nature of the international political process may also present to the Soviets increased opportunities at decreased risks which will be too tempting to pass up. In particular, if world politics is increasingly divided along the North-South axis rather than East-West issues, the Soviet Union may find itself aligning with the Third and Fourth World countries which are demanding a better economic deal from Western Europe and the United States.

The growing importance of North-South issues is, however, more likely to complicate rather than simplify the old pattern of East-West divisions. As the poor countries proceed in the quest for a "new economic order," the ideological inclination of Soviet leaders will be to side with them. Their perceived political interest may also lead them to join the developing countries in a posture of contention with the industrialized non-Communist countries. On the other hand, the Soviet Union will want to export technology and manufactured goods, and will often find itself sharing common interests with the industrial states. And, in a world threatend by nuclear proliferation, the Soviet Union will share with the Western nuclear powers the desire to contain the spread of nuclear weapons within the developing world. The emerging international system will therefore be a complex one, with inter-connected issues and cross-cutting political alignments requiring a degree of coordinated international management hitherto nonexistent. In such an in-terdependent world, the costs and benefits of seizing upon the opportunities created by economic or political difficulties in one camp or the other will have to be carefully weighed, and the edge of the argument may often be on the side of restraint.

Western Europe as a Constraint on Soviet Power

Pierre Hassner

A highly instructive method to evaluate the present European situation is to compare it with the European situation of ten years ago—between the Cuban Missile Crisis and the invasion of Czechoslovakia. At that time, the West did have its problems, represented by America's preoccupation with the Vietnam War and by De Gaulle's challenge to Atlantic solidarity and European integration, and the Soviet Union did maintain her power over Eastern Europe. But America enjoyed unquestioned strategic superiority, Western Europe's economic growth, ideological consensus and political stability seemed unchallenged, whereas the Soviet Union with a collective leadership following a humiliated Khrushchev seemed on the defensive, both domestically and in Eastern Europe. Experts were discussing the "degeneration of the Soviet System" or "the agony of the regime in the Soviet Union." Even more, they were writing about "the break-up of the Soviet Empire in Eastern Europe" and about the irresistible trend towards liberalization and national independence. The question of the day was the evolution of Eastern Europe, the extent to which Soviet-run organizations like Comecon and the Warsaw Pact could accommodate to it, and the extent to which Western policies could or should encourage, steer, or channel it. These were the times of competing plans for an "alternative to partition," for "European reunification," for "peaceful engagement in Eastern Europe," for "building bridges" or for a "Europe from the Atlantic to the Urals."

Today, the tables are turned. One does not hear very much about the future of various East European countries, let alone about the breakdown of the Soviet Empire, because since 1968 the Soviet Union has been remarkably successful in stabilizing her sphere, in clipping the wings of Hungarian reform or Rumanian independence, in promoting integration through a variety of institutional channels. On the other hand, one does hear much speculation about the future of West European countries, of Portugal and Spain, of Greece and Turkey, of Italy and France, about their domestic evolution towards popular fronts or their diplomatic evolution towards non-alignment, about the ability of Western institutions like the Common Market or NATO to accommodate these evolutions, about the Soviet Union's role in instigating, exploiting, moderating or channeling them, in other words about her "peaceful engagement in Western Europe."

This happens within a broader context where, also, the balance of confidence seems to be favoring the East. Economically and ideologically, the crisis of the capitalist system is as spectacular as that of the Communist one, whose sterility seems compensated by a greater stability as well as by a lesser reliance on foreign sources of energy and raw materials. Politically and strategically, the shadow of America's retreat from Vietnam looms as large as that of the retreat of the Soviet missiles from Cuba in the earlier period; the Soviet Union's accession to strategic parity, her conventional build-up in Europe, her new global naval power, contrast with the problems arising for American bases (in particular in a crucial country like Turkey) and, even more, with the unpredictability stemming from the present state of the relations between Congress and the Presidency.

This shift in the general balance is seen by many as being engineered by the Soviet Union (whose hand they see behind the Italian Communists as well as behind the Portuguese ones, behind the oil producers as well as behind the Palestinian terrorists) or as being just one sign of a general historical trend towards the decline of the West, or of the United States, or of capitalism, or of liberal democracy. There may be some truth in both these general, conspiratorial or fatalistic views. Yet the analysis suggested here is both more modest and more differentiated. There have been similar periods, for instance at the end of the 1950s, when Sputnik, Suez, Soviet growth rates, and the spurious missile gap contributed to a feeling that history was favoring the East, only to be followed by the Sino-Soviet split, the troubles of the Communist economies, and the new dynamism of the West under the Kennedy Administration. Moreover, while the results of recent events do favor the Soviet Union and do reveal a deep crisis of existing Western structures and systems, the linkage between the two can by no means be identified. Even if she was marginally involved, the Soviet Union is by no means the main actor in the energy crisis, in Portugal, in the evolution of Italy, let alone in America's self-engineered troubles with Greece and Turkey. Nor is the West's loss necessarily her gain. Capitalism or liberal democracy may decline in favor of right-wing regimes or of national Communist ones which may be even less controlled by the Soviet Union than by the United States or Western Europe.

It is best, then, to look at political developments in various West European countries, at the impact of the economic crisis, and at the presence and role of the superpowers as three separate dimensions whose interaction creates a general balance of direct or indirect West European vulnerability to the Soviet Union.

POLITICAL DEVELOPMENTS

The political evolution of Western Europe must be seen in the light of a complex process of differentiation and interaction between various dimensions of international reality which, during the time of the Cold War proper, tended to be artificially lumped or held together. Until 1968, the coincidence between a country's geographical position, her military and diplomatic alignment, and her domestic political regime was more or less taken for granted. There were some marginal cases—non-Communist or nonaligned neighbors of the Soviet Union, non-democratic regimes in the West—but by and large the East-West division was the commanding factor for a country's orientation.

1968 showed that, under the surface, a social, ideological, and political evolution was taking place which could lead an east-central European country, like Czechoslovakia, to drift away from Soviet Communism and a western country, like France, to be on the verge of revolution. In both cases, the system won the day. But while in the East its victory has been consolidated ever since, in Western Europe the forces for social and political change, which had always had a greater chance to influence political structures and orientations, have increasingly asserted themselves, sometimes by overthrowing, more often by evading the authority and the legitimacy of existing institutions or ruling elites. The causes and the effects of the process vary from country to country: the role of international factors has only been to remove the barriers which the existence of a common enemy (the Soviet Union) and

of a common model or protector (the United States) had provided against
the emergence of differences and conflicts within and between countries.

In France and Italy, détente has legitimized the Communist parties and
has made a left-wing alternative less unthinkable or unacceptable once it no
longer seemed identified with Soviet domination. In Greece and Turkey, the
decline in the possibility of a Soviet threat has encouraged the conflict over
Cyprus which itself has led to the collapse of the Greek dictatorship and to
the deterioration of Turkey's relations with the United States. The change
of regime in Portugal was also made more tolerable, at least in the first place,
by détente. But the actual reasons for these various developments lie in the
domestic dynamics of the various societies: the desire for change after fifteen,
thirty, or fifty years of government without an alternative, or the disruptions
caused by economic modernization, or the revolt against a corrupt and in-
effective dictatorship, or the identity crisis produced by specific national ex-
periences in relation with Islam, Africa, or the Mediterranean World.

Indeed, the most worrisome problem for NATO and the European
Community (which both, especially the latter, require a certain convergence
or compatibility between the domestic regimes of their members) is precisely
the diversity of their situations and orientations. This is best illustrated by a
hypothetical situation in which West Germany would be led by Franz-Josef
Strauss, France led by the left-wing coalition, Italy by a right-wing coup,
England by a left-oriented Labor after having turned its back on the European Community. While some elements of this scenario are still quite possible, so far the trend even in Portugal and Spain has been away from the
dramatic confrontations which were feared in 1975 and toward accommodation. Britain has remained within the Community, the latter has shown signs of
a certain renewal in cohesion and initiative. France and Germany have more
compatible and cooperative leaderships than ever since Adenauer. Chancellor
Schmidt and the Social Democratic Party (S.P.D.) play a positive role in encouraging stability and coordination throughout Western Europe. In Italy the
general crisis does not seem to prevent a certain economic recovery, and the
overdue political change seems to be channeled through peaceful and constructive means, thanks, in particular, to an apparently independent and
pluralistic Communist Party. The declaration of the Italian and Spanish Communist Parties, in July 1975, committing themselves to a specifically Western
type of socialism adapted to the specific social and international situation of
Western Europe, opens a hopeful perspective for the mutual adaptation of

the two essential and often contradictory dimensions of Europe's future: social change and international stability.

But, of course, the Stalinism of the French and Portuguese Communist Parties, the possibility of right-wing reactions to leftward trends even in Italy, and, all the more so, in post-Franco Spain, persisting domestic and external tensions in Greece and Turkey, the possibility of Britain's social and political fabric being torn apart by economic disarray and political polarization in spite of continued membership in the Community, remain sources of worry which make a "best-case scenario" substantially less likely than a "worst-case" one.

THE ECONOMIC CRISIS

Probably the most decisive variable is the outcome of the economic crisis and of its political consequences. Even if the crisis is a transitory one, its consequences can become permanent if it leads to the collapse of fragile regimes or to irreversible changes in their international ties.

One of the most damaging effects of the crisis has been to accentuate the differences between Western European States, thereby making a coordination of social and economic policies both more necessary and more difficult. Hence ideas are generated about a two-tier European community in which a country like the Federal Republic of Germany would have more in common with the United States than with the currently weaker members of the Community, like Britain and Italy. In most countries, except in Germany and to some extent France, the crisis produces an increasing concentration on domestic problems, with a decrease in defense budgets and a decrease in the attention paid to security matters. Another international consequence of inflation and unemployment is an ideological loss of confidence within the East-West debate as the West seems less sure to be affluent while the East appears to guarantee more job security as well as more order in the streets. This should not be exaggerated, however, as the smaller East European countries are also badly affected both by the Western crisis and by the harshness of Soviet treatment regarding the price of energy and raw materials. There are signs of serious discontent within the Soviet bloc in this respect. The real phenomenon is the increasing vulnerability and frustration of small and middle countries in regard to the two superpowers.

Certainly the energy crisis, in particular, has created problems for the Soviet Union and for the United States; but it did even more so for their allies, who have to rely upon the two superpowers to a greater extent than before and hence provide the latter with additional leverage for political use. The crisis has increased both a feeling of European identity and one of European impotence. The small and middle powers of Europe, dependent upon foreign energy sources and incapable of securing their supply by themselves, have discovered both that their interests did not necessarily coincide with those of the United States—let alone of the Soviet Union or of the Third World—yet that they had to rely upon the protection, the toleration, or the goodwill of these external powers.

THE ROLE OF THE SUPERPOWERS

There is an analogy, in terms of comparative vulnerability between the military and the economic dimensions of Europe's security. In both cases, the United States has become vulnerable to a Soviet nuclear attack or to an Arab oil boycott; in both cases, Europe is even more vulnerable and would suffer even more if the worst did happen; but in both cases, it is essentially the United States who has the means to keep the peace and whose relations with the Soviet Union or the Arabs determines the fate of Europe. As it is vulnerable itself, Europe must protect its own interests which cannot be entirely identical with those of its allies, or at least cannot be perceived in identical terms, as far as the acceptance of risks is concerned. Yet the same allies must look upon the United States to protect their interests, or those of the system, as well as its own, unless they try to make their own accommodation with the source of the potential threat, which they can only do, today, from a position of weakness, especially as long as they try to do it separately.

This gives the United States a choice between trying to use the weakness of the Europeans to reassert its leadership or trying to encourage them towards greater self-confidence and self-reliance. The first attitude is, to some extent, inevitable and desirable in the short run, since there is no one else to take the lead and since a reaffirmation of American credibility after Watergate and Vietnam is called for. This is what the Nixon-Kissinger and the Ford-Kissinger Administration have been doing. On the other hand, pushed too far and without being combined with the encouragement of simultaneous independent effort and long-range devolution, it may be self-defeating. The Europeans are too frustrated and their situations (both in terms of subjective feelings and of objective needs) are too diverse to allow them to trust entirely a leader who has, quite legitimately, his own axe to grind.

On the other hand, the leader himself is not able to deliver because of his internal diversions and weaknesses, and is unable to guarantee that transatlantic divergence of interest and perceptions will not, in the long run, increase rather than diminish. Hence, the mixture of cooperation and recrimination which we have witnessed in 1974 and 1975. The balance between the three levels of Western solidarity, of European autonomous unity, and of national diversity and divergences seems extremly hard to manage both for the United States and for its allies—yet it is the contradictions between these levels which, more than anything else, make Western Europe vulnerable to Soviet power.

Mr. Peer H. Lange raised the question: "Could not Soviet efforts in the military fields be aimed at the stimulation of self-weakening processes within the 'imperialist camp' rather than at extorting political gains by direct military threat or use of force."[1] This would be in perfect agreement with Lenin's dictum, recently quoted by a usually authoritative Soviet writer, C. Sanakoev: "Revolutionary political activity consists in using the enemy's policies, especially when these policies are preparing his own destruction."[2]

This notion of Soviet policy, including Soviet military power, playing an active but indirect role, aimed at encouraging existing trends within the West, in particular the contradictions within societies and between states, seems to offer the key to our general problem of Western Europe's vulnerability to Soviet power and, by the same token, the most plausible answer to a number of well-known debates about the character of Soviet policy (expansionist or conservative?), about the Soviet attitude to détente, and about Soviet reactions to the crisis of capitalism and to the prospects for political change in Western Europe.

The most widespread assumption that seems to have been adopted by most Western governments and by the great majority of public opinion in Western Europe is that Soviet intentions, in Europe at least, are essentially conservative and defensive. According to this view, the Soviet Union has become, through the combined effect of ideological erosion, economic progress and needs, the fear of nuclear war, and of its conflict with China a status quo power. Soviet European policy has two fundamental objectives: (1) to preserve its authority in Eastern Europe and (2) to enlist the economic

[1]Peer H. Lange, "Communist Military Political Attitudes," mimeo, Stiftung Wissenschaft und Politik, Munich, 1975.

[2]C. Sanakoev, "The Foreign Policy of Socialism," *International Affairs*, May, 1975. Moscow.

cooperation of Western Europe, particularly of Germany. Its relations with
the two great extra-European powers, the United States and China, reinforce
these trends. It sees China as the main threat and thus wants stability in
Europe and an understanding with the United States, which, by making détente irreversible, would dispel the nightmare of a Sino-American alliance.
Thus it wants neither to engage in any aggressive adventure in Europe,
which would jeopardize détente, nor to encourage a Western European eman-
cipation from the United States which would jeopardize the bipolar status
quo. Its military force, like its diplomacy, is status quo oriented: it is meant
to keep Eastern Europe quiet, to keep the West at bay, and to keep the
Soviet military happy.

As against this, a vocal minority in the West, as well as the official Chinese and Albanian view, claims that Soviet policy is essentially offensive and
expansionist. They base this analysis of Soviet objectives either on the requirements of Leninist ideology (which are being sustained by constant Soviet
references to the international class struggle) or on the tradition of Russian
imperialism. Seen in this perspective, détente is only the continuation of
the cold war by other means. These means are not likely to include direct
military conquest, at least in Western Europe, but they do include the use
of military force, both directly, at lower subconventional levels (subversion,
terrorism, and espionage) and indirectly, at the conventional and nuclear
level. The constant striving of the Soviet Union for military superiority is,
according to this view, aimed essentially at extracting political advantages
from the West, whether in the guise of diplomatic concessions or through
the encouragement of the political and psychological process of "Finlandi-
zation."

While this perspective applies to Soviet foreign policy in general, many
of those who hold this view believe that Western Europe, far from being
a backwater as regards Soviet strategy, is the essential prize, the attainment
of which it is aimed at. Again, the Chinese have been recently lending their
support to this view, at least when talking to Western European statesmen
and encouraging them to resist Soviet expansionism.

SOVIET POLICY OBJECTIVES

In my opinion, these two contrary views both contain an element of truth,
but both can be misleading—precisely because they focus on static and mutually exclusive definitions of ends and means, of motives and strategies.

They both tend to neglect or to minimize what Khrushchev used to call the dynamic character of the status quo, particularly in the present phase of international relations and particularly in Europe, and the necessity of adopting a dialectical approach both in order to grasp it and in order to act upon it. To that extent, the Marxist approach, with its emphasis on helping or hindering historical processes, seems better suited to the present phase of European politics than either a classical approach, whether diplomatic or economic, or a purely ideological one.

In the present circumstances, the Soviet Union is being spared the necessity of choosing between ultimately incompatible goals or strategies, thanks both to the constraints of the status quo and to its evolutionary character. This is the case today more than at other times, in Europe more than in other places, for the Soviet Union more than for other powers.

The two essential characteristics of the Soviet Union, its geopolitical dimensions, as compared, in particular, to those of its European neighbors, and its revolutionary origins, compel it to be in a dynamic relationship with its environment. It is a threat to its neighbors by the sheer weight of its mass. It feels encircled or threatened by them through the very uniqueness of its regime. This is what the discussion about its revolutionary or conservative objectives and about its offensive or defensive policies seems to miss.

Even assuming that the primary goal of the Soviet Union is its economic development, the nature of its regime leads it to conceive this development in terms of a combination of competition with the West ("catching up with the United States"), of cooperation with it (borrowing or learning from the capitalists in order to compete with them) and also, precisely for this reason, of hostile isolation from it in order to avoid ideological contamination and to maintain as much autocracy as possible. This type of development—emphasizing self-reliance, isolation, and power over welfare—necessarily has foreign policy implications, especially for Western European states which have made the opposite choice—of pluralism, prosperity, and permeability. Their inability or unwillingness to constitute a power of comparable dimensions and cohesion puts the Soviet Union in the situation of an "objective Finlandizer."

Conversely, the attraction they may exert towards Eastern Europe, together with the latter's own social and national trends, are considered by the Soviet Union as dangers to its security, which it defines in terms of the security of its authority over its empire. Hence the resort, on its part, to military action, which it understands as defensive, or at least as protective.

But however conservative an interpretation one may put on the intervention in Budapest or in Prague, they—and the Western reactions, or absence thereof—obviously have a demonstrative effect concerning the respective power and resolution of the countries concerned. Hence the confirmation of the status quo in Eastern Europe modifies it in Western Europe. This is why to describe Soviet policy as simply revisionist or expansionist or as bent exclusively on maintaining the status quo is to miss both the essential ambivalence of the status quo and the particular ambivalence of Soviet policy.

Paradoxically, the power relations between Soviet and Western Europe have been more influenced by what happened within the two spheres than by any action, diplomatic or military, directed at one another.

It is the constant implicit and explicit comparison and communicat.vn between the evolution of the two Germanys, the two Europes, the two integrations, the two alliances, the two systems which characterizes, more than ever before and more than anywhere else, the present period in Europe and, I think, its perception by Soviet policy-makers. The essential phenomenon is that of indirect influence, of the demonstrational effect of actions and processes taking place on one side upon the perceptions and attitudes of the other. In Europe today the predominance of this phenomenon, whose substance was aptly characterized by Leopold Labedz with the name "competitive decadence," gives rise to what I have proposed to call a new phase, that of the "hot peace."

HOT PEACE

The characteristics of this phase explain why both schools of Sovietology may be both right and wrong in their interpretation of Soviet policies in Europe. The first has been right so far to point out that we are in a fundamentally new phase which, in a sense, is as distinct from the cold war as the latter is from open war. This new phase is based on the avoidance not only of nuclear war and of a major conventional invasion which might escalate into it, but also of direct threats (as used by Khrushchev in 1957-62) and of the active encouragement of insurrection. Contrary to Khrushchev's frontal assault on the status quo, the policy of the successors does, in accordance with the spirit of the new phase, rest on its acceptance, including, especially since 1969, the existing regimes and economic and military organizations. Secondly, while being based on the division of Europe, the new phase is also based on a fundamental Soviet decision to seek the economic and technological cooperation of the West, particularly of the United States and of West Germany. Hence, the notion of "making détente irreversible" is something more than the classical notion of peaceful coexistence, understood as ideological struggle by every means short of war.

But the pessimist school is right to point out that the new phase is still one of conflict and inequality, of the search for influence and of exploitation of the weaknesses of the other side. It is right to point out that while the new period is based on the acceptance of the status quo, this recognition of realities does not exclude the desire to change them.

On the second point the pessimist school is equally right in pointing out that the desire for technological and economic cooperation does not exclude the need for cultural and ideological isolation, which in turn requires a degree of political hostility. Indeed, the economic opening may even be a result of the refusal or inability to reform the system. The desire for ideological autarky is certainly reinforced by the fears of the results produced by the necessity of abandoning the economic one. The optimist school is probably right in pointing out that the many statements in favor of the intensification of the ideological struggle or of vigilance against imperialism quoted by the pessimist school are probably meant primarily for domestic consumption and are intended to protect Communist rule in the East rather than extend it to the West through any grand plan for subversion. But the optimist school is wrong not to see that precisely this need for defensive hostility means a permanent fragility for this very détente which the Soviet Union tries, for economic reasons, to make irreversible. It means, moreover, that the very acceptance of the risk of détente, in conditions of economic inferiority and ideological vulnerability, leads to a constant need to compensate for these weaknesses by demonstrating superior power, stability and unity. The defensive preoccupation with improving or at least maintaining the status quo in the East (hence with fighting centrifugal trends, like the attraction of the West) implies an offensive preoccupation with controlling the status quo in the West, or at least fighting those trends which might increase its attraction to and influence over the East.

It is true that nobody, including, I think, the Soviet Union, wants a complete breakdown of the other side's structure, organizations, and regimes. But it is precisely once both sides have to some extent accepted each other's realities that the real game of influencing them begins. Because the age of the "hot peace" is the age of mutual vulnerability, the competition is being carried on, much more than before, on the other side's territory; but, conversely, this is done less by intervening there oneself than by exploiting its own contradictions or its own reactions to common challenges.

Like Brandt, Brezhnev has understood that the only way to change the status quo is by accepting it, because it is precisely this acceptance, by the relaxation it provides, which has a chance of unleashing forces of change. The nature of this lies, then, in a competition for the control and the channeling of these forces in exploiting them for one's own advantage without letting them destroy the common structure.

To the extent that the Soviet Union has a strategy, it seems to me to lie in exploiting the inner tensions within Western European states, between them and between Western Europe and the United States, just enough to maintain Eastern superiority in military strength and political unity, but not enough to provoke a collapse with unpredictable social and international consequences. It no longer asks for the complete separation of West Berlin from West Germany, of West Germany from the European Economic Community and NATO, of the United States from Europe. Nor does it, under present circumstances, aim at the breakdown of the social order in European states or at the breakdown of the European Economic Community (EEC). But within existing structures, it aims at a West Berlin as detached as possible from West Germany, a West Germany in as special a position as possible as compared to the rest of Western Europe, a European Community as little integrated as possible, a Western Europe as detached as possible from the United States.

Similarly, the Soviet Union would see more problems than advantages today in a Western Europe collapsing into economic autarky and anarchy, which would deprive it of an economic partner it needs, or led by Communist parties, which could either result in unpredictable American or right-wing reactions, or raise polycentric challenges to Moscow's primacy. But it would like Western Communist parties to exert enough influence, from outside or from within, on bourgeois governments, to influence their foreign policy in favor of East-West détente and against Western and European integration, particularly political and military.

In other words, in the present period characterized by ambiguity and contradictions, by new links between adversaries and new tensions between allies, by the simultaneous and contradictory progress of economic interdependence and economic nationalism, Soviet policy towards Western

Europe seems essentially geared to make the best use possible of these contradictory trends. It seems essentially reactive and preventive, adapting to
realities the Soviet Union has fought, trying to prevent them from developing
in further directions inimical to its interests, trying to use opportunities—
from De Gaulle to the energy crisis, from Portugal to Cyprus—when they
occur.

SOVIET PERCEPTIONS

The Soviet Union sees that three basic changes have occurred in international relations and that they are ushering in a qualitatively new era:
(1) the change in the world balance of power in favor of the socialist camp;
(2) the opening up of cooperative relations between states with different social
systems, especially the United States and the Soviet Union; and (3) the
growth of contradictions within the capitalist camp, especially between the
United States and Western Europe. These three changes are interrelated
and reinforce each other. The change in the balance of power favors détente,
which exacerbates tensions between the United States and Western Europe.
But, if pushed to an extreme, each could have counterproductive effects on
the whole. If the first priority is to maintain Soviet rule in the Soviet Union
itself and in Eastern Europe and the second is to encourage the three above-
mentioned trends and discourage countertrends, any all-out effort for détente,
or for military superiority, or for getting U.S. troops out of Europe has its
dangers if it is not counterbalanced by efforts to prevent, for instance, a
reaction in favor of Western Europe military and political power.

The preferred policy seems rather to keep options open between the
desirable priorities and, conversely, by exercising a discreet leverage on long-
range trends and exploiting tactical opportunities to close as many options
as possible to the other side (like preventing a strong German army or Western
European defense through the CSCE and the Mutual Force Reduction
[MBFR] negotiations and more generally by ensuring the primacy of East-
West ties). Once again, in present conditions, a status quo policy in the
Soviet sense means preventing Western developments which would change
the status quo by altering the balance where it is weighted in favor of the
Soviet Union, such as in the military field. For this, the best solution is a
surviving but weak and disunited Atlantic alliance with an American presence and role insufficient to reestablish Atlantic unity, but enough to keep a
bilateral control and to prevent the emergence of an independent and united

Europe. To this extent, the only way for the Soviet Union to prevent a "status quo *minus*" is to strive, within the framework of an acceptance of existing structures, for a status quo *plus*, which would add to its leverage in the West by the multiplication of East-West bilateral ties and multilateral structures.

CONCLUSIONS

Today, the Soviet Union is able to keep its options open, while striving to decrease the range of options open to Western Europe, precisely because we are in an intermediate phase. The combination of cooperation and hostility with the West, of the desire for technological communication and human isolation does create new dilemmas for the Soviet Union or sharpen old ones; but the combination of stability and crisis in the West enables it, at the political level, to impose its own formula for living with these dilemmas and with some older ones. This is possible only in a contradictory phase like the present one. If the West were either to unite in a common policy or to collapse in a general crisis, the Soviet Union might be forced to make fundamental choices instead of living with compromises and tactical maneuvers which, provisionally, at least, enable it to have its cake and eat it too.

The question is whether, in 1975, we have not reached such a point. Indeed, there were signs that elements of the two opposite situations, a strong West asking for difficult concessions and a collapsing West offering tempting opportunities, were present at the same time—the Jackson amendment for the first, the economic difficulties of the West and the evolution of Mediterranean Europe for the second. The two, combined, must have raised the issue, for Soviet policy-makers, whether some risks concerning détente and cooperation with the West (which was proving less rewarding economically and technologically than expected) were not worth accepting for the sake of an expansion of power and influence in Western Europe. At any rate, during the winter of 1974-75, Soviet policy gave signs of hesitation or wavering that coincided with Brezhnev's illness but also with a number of ambiguous moves (from the cancellation of the Trade Agreement with the United States to the campaign of the French Communists against the Socialists). Each of them could be interpreted in different ways; nor was it certain that they constituted a pattern. Hence, the usual two theories have re-emerged.

For the more optimistic one, the Soviet Union is more embarrassed than anyone else by the new opportunities offered by the Western crisis. She wants above all to save détente and to prevent adventures, hence to preserve the status quo. She is afraid that the crisis may encourage hostile forces in the West, hence the cancellation of the Trade Bill is directed more against Senator Jackson than against détente; a victory of the left in France or Italy might help cold war forces in Germany (like F.J. Strauss) or the United States besides saddling the Communists with responsibility for taking unpopular measures in an unmanageable crisis; hence, by attacking the Socialists as well as by having a dialogue with the right, the aim is to prevent a premature coming to power of the left. For the opposite view, which is gaining ground, on the contrary, the crisis of capitalism, the political opportunities in Western Europe and her own military power induce the Soviet Union to go to the offensive. The more powerful she becomes, the more she tends to discard her usual caution: she supports Idi Amin, sells nuclear reactors to Khadafi, encourages the hard line of the Portuguese Communists and even, perhaps, according to some recent and disturbing evidence, the activities of terrorist groups in the West and the Middle East.

Of course, if one looks to ideological pronouncements, one finds more support for the latter line, as many speeches and articles emphasize the new stage in the crisis of capitalism, the sliding of the European continent to the left, and the possibility of revolutionary developments in several Mediterranean countries. If one looks at diplomatic gestures, the opposite seems to be true. However, even in the doctrinal texts, one finds cautionary words about the dangers of fascism being produced, like in the 1930s, by the alienation of the middle classes, and about the necessity of economic cooperation with the West; on the other hand, neither diplomatic caution nor preoccupation with détente seem to have prevented the Soviet Union from a much more active and intransigent role in Portugal than was usually expected, not to speak of their new global threat evidenced by their role in Angola.

As usual, a clear-cut choice between opposing interpretations is difficult; again, a combination of the two seems in order. The Soviet Union continues to try to have her cake and eat it too, and to avoid hard choices. Where these seem inevitable, they will be determined both by an evaluation of likely reactions in the West and of the specific local circumstances. Almost universally, her initial reaction to new opportunities is one of extreme caution and distrust of the unknown. But when the trend is confirmed, as well as the inability of the West to solve its problems, she starts exploiting it, not by abandoning détente and cooperation but by suggesting that they ought to take into account the fact that she has an alternative option, and that the "correlation of forces" has changed. But she still acts very differently in cases like Portugal (whose loss she feels may be accepted by the West without jeopardizing détente and whose Communist Party is particularly faithful) and one like Italy, where the P.C.I. acceding to power may provoke more dangerous reactions in the West yet be less easy to control and more likely to cause trouble for the Soviet Union itself.

Perhaps the United States and Western Europe would be well-advised to follow this example. On the one hand, the link between détente and the existing balance should be made crystal clear to the Soviet Union, who should not be allowed to get symbolic (like in Helsinki) or economic help while expanding militarily or diplomatically at the expense of the West; but on the other hand the utmost flexibility is required for the various regional and national crisis whose outcome may or may not result in such advantages for the East. Nothing could give the Soviet Union a more easy and less risky victory—for instance in Italy or Spain—than the United States or Western Europe choosing to inflict defeat upon themselves by choosing the losing side or interpreting ambiguous developments as directed against them. In the last analysis, our worst vulnerabilities to Soviet power are those we bring about ourselves.

Ostpolitik and the Present State and Future Course of Inner-German Contacts

The purpose of this paper is to examine the implications of West Germany's Ostpolitik for the political legitimacy and stability in Eastern Europe, and then to analyze the current level of contacts between the two German states and the future of this unprecedented relationship. It starts from several basic propositions: (1) in the 1960s the German question was the heart of the Soviet Union's security problem in Europe; (2) the new "Brandt Ostpolitik since 1969 (as differentiated from Erhardt's "New Opening" and Kissinger's new Eastern policy) is a profound expression of the détente process between the Soviet Union and the United States, and, as such, has broad ramifications for Eastern Europe; (3) the Soviet involvement in the "Ostpolitik process" of political adjustment is multidimensional: it is based on the concepts of internationalism, security, and stability required by the USSR as vital to its national interests, and, therefore, subject only to the most cautious alteration; (4) internationalism necessitates Eastern European acceptance of Soviet leadership in domestic and foreign affairs, and legitimacy entails acceptance of the Soviet formula establishing political authority through the concepts of minority rule by the Communist Party and democratic centralism in all decision-making unmolested by external influences. The aggregation of these multidimensional aspects of Ostpolitik have had both a stabilizing and a corrosive effect on Eastern Europe.

DEVELOPMENT OF OSTPOLITIK

The package of treaties negotiated between the FRG and the USSR, Poland, and the German Democratic Republic (GDR) in 1969-1972, known collectively as the "Ostvertraege," extended West German recognition of the territorial status quo in Eastern Europe; an act reaffirmed in the Helsinki Final Protocol of the CSCE conference. The Ostvertraege and the CSCE agreement did not prohibit or reduce Western influence in Eastern Europe. Rather, they altered the quality of Western interests in the nature of change in Eastern Europe, i.e., they indicated that the West was becoming increasingly committed to the modernization of the socialist states. Nonetheless, they provided a new sense of stability for both the Eastern Europeans and the Soviets, based on Western recognition of the existing status quo. However, the durability of this element of stability provided by the West may be compromised by other eroding elements of Ostpolitik and increased contact with the West. The issue of Ostpolitik itself, and the resolution of the German problem introduced division and dissent into the Warsaw Pact. As late as 1966 there was no unified Pact policy on the German question. By 1967 the papered-over fissures were exposed by Rumania's adoption of a two Germanys policy and its establishment of diplomatic relations with Bonn. Economic contacts between the FRG and most Eastern European countries expanded steadily during this period. The result was a major Pact crisis over the German issue, and a polarization of the member states between Rumania's independent position and the GDR's espousal of the Ulbricht Doctrine which prohibits diplomatic recognition of the FRG by any Socialist state until Bonn establishes full relations with East Berlin. Between these extremes, the Eastern European pursued their respective national interests vis-à-vis Bonn, albeit in close synchronization with Soviet policy, as evidenced in May 1969 when Poland's Gemulka, without prior consultations with Ulbricht, publicly offered to negotiate with the Federal Republic over the Oder-Neisse line.

Thus, erosions in Socialist unity emerged as the individual members sought resolution of their respective national grievances against the Germans or autonomous policies, i.e., Czechoslovakia, Rumania, and Yugoslavia. But, the divisive effect of the German issue and national autonomy during the throes of Ostpolitik seemed to partially recede after the conclusion of each step toward "normalization." The result of this "controlled flux" in the policies of Pact members was that the USSR recognized the necessity of adopting a new Eastern European policy based on flexibility, caution, and strength.

CHANGE IN SOVIET POLICY

This modification of policy resulted, paradoxically, in both a narrowing and broadening of Soviet margins of tolerance. The narrowing of Soviet policy, especially after 1969 was first demonstrated by the imposition of tighter ideological controls over the Pact members. Second, regional integration was accelerated. Third, Eastern European countries became increasingly dependent upon the USSR for raw materials as world prices rose much faster than those of the Soviet Union. And finally, the military proficiency and weapons modernization rates of the Eastern European forces substantially improved.

The broadening aspects of Soviet policy, on the other hand, were characterized in two ways. First the USSR, like the West, became increasingly conscious of the need to accelerate the modernization process among all Socialist states, including itself. The need for modernization tended to emphasize the different levels of development of each Socialist state, and to accentuate their respective societal requirements. This led to the second factor: the gradual modification of the socioeconomic structure of Eastern Europe, characterized by increased consumerism and modest reforms. While the Soviet model for planned socialist progress was still ubiquitous, the mounting complexity of this progress itself required greater Soviet tolerance for moderate national deviations; from privately owned land in Poland in constitutional reforms in Hungary. Indeed, in 1970-71 Rumania and Hungary joined GATT, WHO, and FAO, and Rumania obtained preferential tariff status from the Common Market and posed at the UN as a "semi-nonaligned state." Moscow's acceptance of this broader flexibility in national policies of Pact members was because it was naturally contained within the barriers of interdependence imposed by the narrowing of Soviet policy in the above mentioned categories.

There are practical examples of this simultaneous broadening and narrowing of Soviet policy. From 1960 on, trade among COMECON nations, with the exception of Rumania, steadily increased. But in the period from 1960-1972 trade between Eastern Europe and the West quadrupled, from $3 billion dollars to $12 billion. A consequence of this economic development is that the more technically advanced Socialist countries are today becoming increasingly dependent on the West in selected industries. The GDR, for exampe, is heavily committed to imports from Western Europe of synthetic rubber, plastics, copper, crude oil, and other raw materials. The volume of trade and its concentration in specific sectors indicates that many COMECON countries are also becoming gradually independent of their traditional sources of supply in Socialist countries at the same time that integration is accelerating.

IMPACT ON REGIONAL STABILITY

The question now arises of how to evaluate these developments in terms of stability in Eastern Europe. On the one hand, there is undoubtedly more security today, from the Russian viewpoint, than ever before, in terms of military, ideological, and political control. On the other hand, there is still a high potential for instability because of the different degrees of socioeconomic development in the various Socialist countries. Thus, variegated development underscores the unsolved problem of legitimacy; a continuing source of instability. The issue of legitimacy is probably most critical in the economically most advanced Eastern European country, the GDR. Both the people and the ruling elite still look to the Federal Republic for recognition and legitimization of their particular form of social development. The GDR still feels compelled to justify its actions by constant and voluminous comparisons with the FRG. The GDR experience with legitimacy has undoubtedly had a profound influence on the sense of stability throughout Eastern Europe.

There is the phenomenon that might be called "ersatz legitimacy," whereby raising the GDR standard of living 30-35 percent above that of the USSR or Czechoslovakia, is cited as evidence of the system's effectiveness. Yet even this ersatz phenomenon lacks the natural basis of genuine legitimacy, namely a national self-identity that exists in Poland, for example. National identity among other Eastern European societies has led to a strong new wave of nationalism, which, partly for the sake of legitimization, may reduce the pace of integration and inhibit Western contacts under détente.

In general, it seems evident that Ostpolitik has increased the competitive tendencies among the Eastern European countries, with the exception of Albania and Bulgaria. They compete among each other for scarce Western credits and markets, and for acceleration of their respective national campaigns for modernization. Such competition, however, is carefully monitored and contained with Moscow's minimum levels of tolerance.

It is also evident that Ostpolitik and détente precipitated a general increase in political vigilance, pressures indicating the unyielding determination of the USSR to protect its hegemonial position even at the risk of slowing down the momentum of East-West accommodation in Europe. The intensified campaign against ideological coexistence suggests a lingering Soviet apprehension and anxiety about the political implications of Ostpolitik, especially on the issues of legitimacy and stability. Or the positive side, however, while Ostpolitik has not succeeded in solving the German question, it has safely relegated the issue to the relatively insulated arena known as the inner-German dialogue.

TOWARD INNER-GERMAN ACCOMMODATION

Present tendencies in international politics towards détente on the basis of the status quo have permitted the two states, the FRG and the GDR, a neighborly spirit of coexistence and cooperation. This development was furthered by the FRG-GDR Basic Treaty (Grundlagenvertrag) of 1972, an integral aspect of the broader outline of Ostpolitik. The treaties with Poland and the Soviet Union provided the legal parameters for the following inner-German negotiations. They were the renunciation of force, the border regulations, and the non-affecting clause (Nichtberuehrungsklausel); i.e., the proviso that relevant agreements which were signed earlier remain unaffected by the new treaties.

The most spectacular events of the inner-German dialogue were the Erfurt and Kassel meetings between former Chancellor Willy Brandt and the former head of the GDR Council of Ministers Willi Stoph in March and May of 1970, respectively. Simultaneously the four-power negotiations on Berlin were begun in March 1970. The results of the Berlin negotiations helped to bring about first, the FRG-GDR Traffic Treaty (26 May 1972) and then, the Basic Treaty.

On 21 June 1973, the Basic Treaty came into force. This treaty provided the basis on which to conduct further negotiations. Both parties, the FRG and GDR, recognized that significant difficulties remained to be settled in the future; over time it would consequently take on fuller and more concrete significance. It follows, therefore, that the negotiations following and supplementing the Basic Treaty are highly pertinent to an evaluation of the treaty itself.

The Basic Treaty may be called a modus vivendi treaty. This means that like all international agreements, it includes some specified principles (e.g., the invulnerability of the borders), but in addition, it provides only a general (minimum) framework for the regulation of the inner-German relations. This framework is functionally dependent on the international political situation, and, in particular, upon the political climate existent between the Soviet Union and the United States.

It should already be clear from these initial observations that the Basic Treaty does not present a final solution for the post-World War II German question. The German question was explicitly kept open in the Treaty and in the accompanying letter regarding the disagreement concerning German unification ("Brief zur Deutschen Einheit") i.e., reunification would be considered in conjunction with the settlement of the division of Europe. Thus, the Four-Power responsibilities concerning Germany are still in effect.

In July 1973 the Federal Constitutional Court published its interpretation of the Basic Treaty, which has had and will continue to have a great impact on the shaping of inner-German relations. By and large, the Court's decision strengthens the FRG in its negotiating positions vis-à-vis the GDR by allowing a certain flexibility and tactical maneuverability in negotiations. Although the Court insisted that all agreements with the GDR comply with the Basic Law of the Federal Republic (Grundgesetz), its ruling left room for interpretation as far as practical details are concerned.

THE PRESENT STATE—INNER-GERMAN CONTACTS

The present relationship between the two German states is characterized by both demarcation and cooperation. The simultaneous presence of these two tendencies is very much in evidence in the political behavior of both states. The most important principles of Brandt's Ostpolitik continue to shape policy under the new Chancellor, Helmut Schmidt. These principles are: the recognition of the status quo; the renunciation of force; the acceptance of the GDR by the FRG as an equal partner in international affairs; the

---

[1]The author wishes to thank the Federal Minister of Inner-German Relations, which provided the figures and statistics cited below.

understanding that the German question be left undecided until an international peace treaty is agreed upon.

The principles laid down in the Basic Treaty provide the grounds on which present contacts between the two German states have been conducted and expanded. Six types of inner-German activities can be distinguished:

1. Permanent and direct plenipotentiary contacts between Undersecretary of State Gunther Gaus and the GDR Deputy Minister for Foreign Affairs Kurt Nier through the West German mission in East Berlin, and reciprocal contacts between the GDR representatives in Bonn, and Dr. Michael Kohl, accredited to the Chancellery (but not the Foreign Office). Gaus and Nier are presently negotiating the following issues, proposed by the GDR in December 1974:

- Cancellation of the requirement that West German and West Berlin citizens of retirement age, upon entry into the GDR, exchange twice the amount of money (as originally agreed upon) from West German to East German marks.
- Improved possibilities for West Berliners to travel within the GDR (at present their visits are restricted to one Bezirk).
- A more lenient handling of requests on the part of West Germans regarding the use of their cars while visiting in the GDR.
- The reopening of the Teltow Canal in Berlin.
- A new Reichsbahn time-table which would facilitate the more efficient and more rapid movement of trains from the FRG to West Berlin.
- Permission for West Germany to build an Autobahn from Hamburg to Berlin.
- An East German contribution to the supply of electricity for West Berlin.
- An East German commitment to buy more machinery from West Berlin.
- GDR preparedness to dispose of additional sewage and garbage produced in West Berlin.
- Offers by West German industry to build a nuclear energy plant in the GDR.
- Offers for jointly developed projects involving individual West German industrial corporations, particularly Krupp and Hoechst.

2. Negotiations on the ministerial level on various matters, e.g., environmental protection.

3. Negotiations on a nongovernmental level, e.g., sports.

4.   Negotiations by the three permanent commissions which were institutionalized in accordance with the treaties signed so far, i.e., the border commission, the transit commission, and the transportation commission. The responsibilities of these commissions were designated as follows: the border commission is to be enhanced by the establishment of fourteen border information offices which will be set up at crossing points into the GDR; the transit commission is to adjudicate differences arising in conjunction with the application of rules set down in the transit protocol pertaining to personal travel; the transportation commission is to rule on problems with reference to that specific treaty.

5.   Contacts through officially accredited journalists (at present: five in Bonn, twelve in East Berlin, sixteen yet to be determined).

6.   Inner-German tourist traffic.[2]

RECENT FRG-GDR NEGOTIATIONS

The following supplementary agreements have been signed subsequent to the date the Basic Treaty went into effect.

1.   20 September 1973:   Agreement concerning the principles for controlling environmental damage and concerning frontier waters.
2.   14 March 1974:   Protocol on the establishment of the permanent missions representing the governments of the FRG and the GDR.
3.   25 April 1974:   Agreement on money transfer in special cases, such as money for child support. The transfer of DM 200.00 per month is permitted in either direction, for a total yearly limit of 30 million DM.
4.   25 April 1974:   Agreement on public health. This accord also involved West Berlin, and, among other things, provides for an extensive exchange of information concerning prophylaxis and control of contagious diseases, and for cooperation in matters of drug abuse (soft and hard drugs). Furthermore, under this agreement

[2]Tourism may be the most important factor in improving contacts. In the period 1972-75 more than 34 million West Germans and West Berliners crossed from the FRG to East Berlin. (This figure is 60 percent higher than the figure for the 1970–72 period). In the first three months of 1975, 700,000 FRG citizens traveled to the GDR. This compares to a figure of 300,000 for 1974, and a total figure of 9.5 million for the time period June 1972–July 1975. Additionally, there was a considerable increase in the number of older citizens traveling from the GDR to the FRG (the figure for 1974 was 1,320,000).

tourists are entitled to free medical care in the guest country, and the exchange of medical drugs is regulated.

5. 8 May 1974:   Agreement concerning the regulations of sports relations between the West German and the East German Sports Federations. This accord explicitly includes West Berlin. The negotiations concerning sports exchanges are nevertheless not to be conducted at the governmental level.

6. 29 June 1974:   Protocol designating the borderline of the Baltic seacoast of the GDR.

7. 29 June 1974:   Protocol notes on fishing rights in the Lübecker Bucht.

The following negotiations are still in progress:

1. On Postal and telephone matters: Postal and telephone matters were negotiated already in 1970 and 1971. They were again raised in 1973. In early 1975 almost 280 telephone wires between the FRG and the GDR were in service and many points in the GDR could be reached by self-dialed calls. In 1974 the Bundespost statisticians registered nearly 4 million telephone calls from the FRG to the GDR. At the end of April 1975, 305 automatic telephone wires were in service between FRG and East Berlin (additionally seventy-six telephone wires were in use between West Berlin and the GDR). The total calls from the FRG and West Berlin to East Berlin and the GDR amounted to 6.1 million in 1974. At present, 126 telex lines are in service between the FRG and West Berlin, and the GDR and East Berlin. Mail flow (letters and parcels) has been speeded up, although it still does not compare with the rapidity of mail transfer within the FRG or between the FRG and France. The technical negotiations improving these services were concluded in May 1975. The question of the incorporation of West Berlin into the intended agreement remains open, since it involves political considerations. It can only be settled by a decision among top-level officials.

2. Negotiations on judicial matters (begun in August 1973):   The outstanding problem area involves relations at the local level (between cities in the FRG and the GDR). The GDR refuses to establish such relations for ideological, organizational, and political reasons. In contrast to the federal system of the FRG, the GDR is a

centralized political system. A second problem is the matter of citizenship. The GDR asserts that there exist two German citizenships. The FRG claims the contrary: that there is only one German citizenship. A third stumbling block in negotiations concerns inter-office assistance (Amtshilfe). This problem has existed for years. It involves questions of the legal rights of citizens who have fled from the GDR, and it includes matters of juvenile status and entitlement to social welfare and insurance coverage. A fourth difficulty involves problems concerning the criminal and civil law in the two German states. In this area there is progress to report. Two groups recruited from both Germanies, one established at the end of 1974, the other in May 1975, work on these problems and appear to be making progress.

3. Economic negotiations: In general, this dimension of East-West German negotiations is proceeding well. Two problem areas should be distinguished; the inner-German trade, and the so-called "swing trade," i.e., FRG interest-free credit to the GDR. Goods traded between East and West Germany amounted to 7 billion marks in 1974 and will probably increase to 7.2-7.5 billion marks in 1975. The swing was raised to 850 million marks per year for the period 1975-1981.

4. Cultural exchanges: The matter of cultural exchanges between the two German states rests on the applications of the CSCE obligations. The final position of the GDR government is yet unclear. The West remains skeptical given the probability that despite the favorable climate of the Helsinki talks, the SED leadership will attempt to avoid an expansion in East-West contacts at the cultural level.

5. Science and technology: In principle, the problems involved in agreements on matters of science and technology are identical to those entailed in cultural exchange matters. The West Germans are still waiting for the GDR to draw appropriate conclusions from the CSCE agreements. The crucial point here again is the inclusion of West Berlin into future accords. In Bonn, prospects for agreement on the exchange of science and technology are considered more promising than in cultural affairs, since it is assumed that the GDR is vitally interested in the former areas.

6. Environmental affairs: Negotiations concerning environmental

affairs, after a promising start, have since reached a deadlock. One reason for this is, again, the West Berlin question. A second reason, however, may be more significant. The GDR is afraid of the costs involved, although only those matters that concern the borderlands are subject to negotiation. Furthermore, the GDR fears that through an agreement on environmental protection, the FRG may gain access to critical information regarding the GDR's economic structure and problems. An additional consideration is that the GDR generally has lower standards than the FRG concerning measures of environmental pollution.

FORMS, CHANCES, AND LIMITS OF INTERSYSTEM COOPERATION

For the purpose of estimating chances, risks, and limitations of the FRG-GDR intersystem cooperation, it is necessary to lay out the assumptions and intentions of our analysis. This, of course, is of particular importance when dealing with the complex fields of humanitarian, economic, cultural, and political cooperation.

Within the context of future possibilities and risks entailed in East-West cooperation, we must proceed from the assumption that the major goal of Soviet policies towards the West is essentially one of weakening the West, and that Soviet offers for cooperation, particularly in the economic and technological field, remain a function of this overall goal. The same assumption holds—to even a more pronounced degree—for the GDR's "Westpolitik."

Since this is the case, the West should be realistic as to what can be derived from and achieved through détente. This requires becoming cognizant of the specific purposes and interests to be served via negotiated cooperation with the East. In determining and ordering our purposes, priorities, and interests, the FRG must calculate not only on the basis of its own interests, but additionally on the interests of the alliances to which it is committed. Within this framework the FRG pursues the following purposes vis-à-vis the GDR: (1) to keep the German question open; (2) to establish a high level of information and communication channels; (3) to provide the GDR with "sufficient" (sufficient in terms of politics) economic aid; (4) to achieve that critical balance of cooperation and demarcation with respect to the GDR for the purpose of further developing the social and economic structure of

West Germany. This involves questions not only of economic standards but of morale as well.

Judging from the groundwork that has been established by the Basic Treaty and the supplementary protocols, we can assume that the FRG and the GDR will continue to negotiate a wide range of issues. In principle such negotiations could cover humanitarian, economic, cultural, and scientific-technological matters, but it is unlikely that negotiations will extend to the political sphere proper—at least in the foreseeable future.

We must, however, keep in mind that all future inner-German cooperation, its contents and forms, is, to a significant degree, dependent upon the progress of the U.S.-USSR détente policies; particularly on the application of CSCE obligations. Thus, the specific effect of détente on future inner-German relations cannot as yet be foreseen. Nevertheless, there are some positive indications.

In recent months the GDR has displayed a much more sober attitude and has been more prepared to compromise in its relations with the FRG. This is due chiefly to economic reasons. After Schmidt's visit to Moscow in November 1974 the GDR became more open-minded because of political pressures from Moscow. (However in April 1975, together with Moscow, East Berlin again hardened its position on West Berlin). After the talks between Chancellor Helmut Schmidt and SED Chief Erich Honecker on the occasion of the 1975 Helsinki CSCE summit, the chances for further negotiations improved. Retarding factors, however, should also be noted. One of these problems is the GDR's balance of payments. East Germany is at present in debt to the industrialized countries of the West for a total of 3.3 billion valuta marks, including approximately 2.2 billion marks credited by the FRG.

POSSIBLE DEVELOPMENTS IN ECONOMIC AND TECHNOLOGICAL AFFAIRS

An abstract analysis of the forms of cooperation is of questionable value. Forms are linked to contents and they change in accordance with differing circumstances. In the context of this analysis, however, we should recognize three distinguishable forms of intersystem cooperation.

1. Direct contacts through the FRG mission in East Berlin and the

GDR representative in Bonn.
2. Negotiations on the governmental level (e.g., supplementary protocols).
3. Negotiations on the nongovernmental level (e.g., sports).

Of the three, the last-named form appears to be the most promising. Following on the sports negotiations, other areas may be brought to conference tables.

Although such contacts on a nongovernmental level can only be established after preliminary, if limited, agreements on the governmental level have been reached, we may realistically anticipate such possible developments, such as:

1. Direct contacts between industrial plants, which may result in cooperation on the production level and in import-export activities from the FRG to the GDR, as well as from one or both German states to third markets, especially in Africa.
2. Some forms of cooperation by multinational corporations on the plant level (e.g., among the FRG, the GDR, and the USSR) may be realized.
3. What holds for the economic sector may also materialize in the field of technological development. This, of course, does not include the area of military technology.
4. Scientific institutes and technical colleges may exchange research results, organize common conferences, and invite scholars from the other state for teaching and research activities. In this context the following disciplines would be involved: medicine, the natural sciences, and the engineering sciences. Furthermore, there is the possibility that for certain commemoration days (which are celebrated in both countries) all-German symposia and congresses could be organized.

All these activities are confined within certain limits. Such limits are set, above all, by the global détente policies. They are further set by the commitments which both German states have made to their individual political and economic allies, and by the domestic situations in both the FRG and the GDR. In other words, besides détente, the political, socio-economic, and ideological factors of both countries have to be taken into account. This point deserves special emphasis in the present period of economic difficulties.

Highly important to technological and scientific cooperation is a proper motivation or interest. In the coming months and years, price increases and the scarcity of raw materials may result in such motivation on the part of the East Germans, and thereby lead the two German states to closer cooperation. On the West German side we can identify the following interests in further cooperation: to maintain and add to the existing contacts with the GDR; to become informed about the scientific and technological level in the GDR; to prepare the West German industry for competition with the East on the world markets.

SOME POSSIBILITIES FOR COOPERATION IN HUMANITARIAN AND CULTURAL AFFAIRS

Cooperation in humanitarian affairs includes the following activities:

1. The bringing together of families separated by the division of the two Germanies. (In 1975 approximately 3,000 such cases were settled.)
2. The care for prisoners. (In 1975 the GDR had about 12,000 citizens in jail on political charges. Two to three thousand are to be released per year because the FRG assumes payment of the fines imposed.)
3. Quick and effective measures to meet accidents at the borderline, especially in Berlin. (On this issue, the GDR insists that the West Berlin Senate must first recognize the bordering that runs through the city of Berlin as the GDR state border.)
4. An increasing number of travel permits for GDR citizens to visit West Germany and permission to emigrate from the GDR to the FRG.

As mentioned above, progress in inner-German cultural affairs depends mainly on the implementation of the CSCE principles. In addition, the issue of competence has to be settled. The GDR wishes to organize its cultural exchange with the FRG through its Ministry of Foreign Affairs, while the FRG stresses the special character of these relations and wants to keep them separated from its foreign relations and handled at the nongovernmental level. In concrete terms, cultural cooperation could be negotiated for the fields of music, literature, theater, and ballet. Books and periodicals could be exchanged, archives could be made accessible, and contacts between museums could be established.

Since 1971, activities in all these fields have increased incrementally. GDR orchestras performed in the FRG, East German writers (e.g. Stefan Heym and Hermann Kant) lectured in the FRG and in West Berlin. As for the book exchanges, since 1971 the average yearly total of books imported and exported amounted to nearly 30 million marks. This figure could be increased considerably. The GDR has been represented for years at the international book fair that takes place annually in Frankfurt/Main. In addition, the writers' union in both Germanies could intensify the existing contacts and stimulate new activities. The same holds for the PEN centers that exist in the FRG as well as in the GDR.

THE QUESTION OF POLITICAL COOPERATION

As suggested earlier, the possibilities for political cooperation are almost nonexistent. The interests of the two German states diverge radically. This is apparent from the fact that while the GDR wants to multilateralize all questions concerning the divided nation, the FRG seeks mainly bilateral contacts.

Despite this state of affairs, during the 29th United Nations General Assembly in 1974 some promising contacts in matters of developmenttal aid were established between the two German delegations. The occasion of these contacts was the issue of making the GDR aware of its responsibilities as an industrial country, and to include it into the bloc of "donor" countries. Such relations could be improved. Within the near future, however, East Germany's development into the functional role of a self-reliant member of the UN is not likely. The close links between GDR and Soviet UN policies do not permit such an eventuality.

CONCLUSIONS

The observations above lead to the realization that at present there is no indication that a far reaching inner-German program or vision exists. At present, and in the foreseeable future, inner-German relations will mainly consist of step-by-step negotiations. This state of affairs makes for an operating understanding from which reunification plans by either side are excluded. Nevertheless, the recent negotiations have taught the FRG how the GDR interprets the meanings of "coexistence" and "cooperation." This

lesson has contributed to the fact that the FRG—and the West in general—
has begun to develop its own political-strategic concept of intersystem coexistence and cooperation.

The Decline of Soviet Influence in the Middle East

William E. Griffith

Until August of 1972, the Soviets had air and naval bases in Egypt and were by far the most important foreign power in Syria and Iraq, while the United States was almost wholly identified with, and its influence largely confined to Israel. Today Soviet influence is still extensive only in South Yemen and to some extent in Libya and Somalia, while American influence in the Arab world has grown greatly, notably in Egypt, and Washington has become the active, "even-handed" mediator between Israelis and Arabs. This diplomatic revolution, albeit perhaps only a temporary one, is as of October 1975 Moscow's greatest political defeat, and Washington's greatest political victory, since the Sino-Soviet split.[1]

[1]This paper is primarily based on travels in the Middle East in July and August, 1975. For background and bibliography, which in general I have not repeated, but only updated, in these footnotes, see my "The Middle East: From the Last War to the Next One," M.I.T. Center for International Studies, C/75-10, mimeo., April 15, 1975, published as "Le Moyen-Orient: avant la prochaine guerre," *Politique étrangère*, no. 2, (1975), pp. 117-140. For general surveys, see Oles M. Smolansky, *The Soviet Union and the Arab East under Khrushchev* (Lewisburg, Pennsylvania: Bucknell University Press, 1974) and "The Soviet Union and the Middle East: The Post-October Period," *Current History*, vol. 69 (October 1975); Robert O. Freedman, *Soviet Policy toward the Middle East since 1970*, (New York: Praeger, 1975); and John K. Cooley, "The Shifting Sands of Arab Communism," *Problems of Communism*, vol. 24, no. 2 (March-April 1975), pp. 22-42.

The extent and causes of the decline of Soviet influence in the Middle East are still far from understood or appreciated in the West. This essay tries to set forth how and why it occurred, estimates its future prospects, and discusses their implications for U.S. foreign policy.

THE HISTORICAL BACKGROUND

Modern Russia has expanded southward as well as to the east and west. The Tsars supported such pre-1914 pan-Slavist "national liberation movements" as the Serb attempt to subvert monarchical Austria-Hungary, in order to unite all South Slavs. The Soviet Union has added a Leninist ideological component: the use of Arab anti-colonialism, anti-Westernism, and leftism to replace Western oriented governments with radical and eventually communist regimes. Like the Tsars it has also dealt with ideologically different movements, e.g., Nasser and the Ba'ath. Moreover, the Soviet global drive for military and naval parity with the United States has made Moscow anxious to gain footholds in the Middle East to aid its navy in the Mediterranean and the Indian Ocean. It also wants to prevent China from penetrating the Middle East. Khrushchev's aims were largely defensive, to leap over the U.S.-forged "northern tier" of Turkey, Iran, and Pakistan and to outflank the U.S. Sixth Fleet and Polaris deployment in the Mediterranean. But, as so often is the case in history, yesterday's defense became today's expansion. Moscow wanted Middle Eastern bases, political influence, and access to oil.

Until 1972 Moscow had three great cards in the Middle East: Arab anti-Westernism, Arab desire to destroy the "expansionist U.S. imperialist outpost" Israel, and Arab Leftists' sympathy for Socialism. Moscow's main weapons were massive arms aid, which the Arabs had to have if they were to fight U.S.-armed Israel, and economic aid for projects such as the Aswan High Dam, which the United States had refused to finance. Moscow's influence reached its peak in 1970, when Israel began deep penetration air raids on

I am grateful to Robert Lewis and Edward Thompson, Jr., of *The Reader's Digest*, which sponsored my summer trip; to Nazli Choucri, John Field, and Oles M. Smolansky, who gave me the benefit of their comments on an earlier draft of this paper; and to all those to whom I talked in the Middle East and elsewhere, whose number and positions lead me not to list them by name.

The first draft of this paper was written in August 1975 when I was a resident scholar at the Rockefeller Foundation's Bellagio Study and Conference Center at Villa Serbelloni (Como.) I am grateful to the Foundation and to the Center's director, Dr. William Olson, and his wife Betsy, for making it so inviting to recall Middle Eastern emotions in Serbelloni's tranquility.

Cairo and Alexandria, to stop Egyptian raids across the Suez Canal and also to try to overthrow Nasser, whose position was already shaky as a result of his crushing defeat by Israel in the 1967 war. To save himself Nasser persuaded the Soviets to send some 20,000 air and naval personnel into Egypt, which deterred Israel from continuing the raids. It seemed that Brezhnev had finally fulfilled the dreams of the Tsars: permanent Russian bases on the Mediterranean and in the Arab East.

THE CAUSES OF THE SOVIET DEFEATS

In August 1972 Nasser's successor, Sadat, threw out most of the Soviet military personnel. By mid-1975, after the 1973 Arab-Israeli war, the Soviet position in Egypt was minimal and American influence far greater. Soviet influence in Syria, never as dominant as usually believed in the West, was also less strong. Recently, and as yet hardly realized in the West, Soviet influence in Iraq has considerably declined. How and why did this all happen?

Even in the Arab world, where the Arab-Israeli issue is so pervasive and corrosive, internal developments usually determine foreign policy. The most important of these has been the economic failure of Nasser's model of socialism in Egypt. Far from solving the economic and social problems of the country, it probably worsened them, or so most of the Egyptian elite thought by the time Nasser suddenly died in 1970. Nasser greatly reduced ostentatious wealth and increased social mobility. But, his bureaucracy was large, inefficient and corrupt; his secret police were omnipresent and brutal; and the population explosion, which might well have doomed any hope for economic development, doomed his "Arab Socialism." In foreign affairs, his long, costly, bloody, and unsuccessful war in the Yemen alienated his military, his people, Saudi Arabia, and many other Arab states as well.

The Soviets also made some major blunders in Egypt. The more the Egyptian intelligentsia and army officers came to know them, the more they saw the Soviets as technologically and culturally inferior Westerners. To the Egyptians, Soviet technology was inferior to that of America and West Germany. The Russian cultural level was very inferior to the French and the British, the traditional models of the Egyption elite, and even to the Americans. Soviet arrogance (the Egyptian Chief of Staff was once refused admission to a Soviet base in Egypt) was worse than the British.

For Sadat eight other factors were also important. First, he was both more of a Muslim and more moderate than Nasser, and he was convinced that the Egyptian economy could only be revived by vast inputs of Western credits and technology. Second, he could get money for arms and investment only from the oil-rich Arab Gulf states, which were conservative, anti-Communist, and anti-Soviet. Third, these states had so much money, after oil prices quadrupled, that they could afford, and decided, to buy him out gradually from under total dependence on Soviet arms supply. Fourth, because they had so much money, and gave Sadat so much to buy arms, the Soviets would no longer give him arms but insisted that he pay for them in hard currency. But because he had to pay for them anyway, and since his moneygivers were anti-Soviet, and since Western arms technology was better than Soviet, why should he maintain his primary alliance with Moscow? Fifth, the Soviets would not sell him their best fighter planes, and they would not fight alongside the Egyptians against Israel. Indeed, in July 1971 the Israeli Air Force deliberately entrapped some Soviet planes into air combat west of the Suez Canal and shot down five in half an hour. The Soviets broke off the combat and never resumed it. Moreover, the Soviet inaction to the American bombing and mining of Hanoi and Haiphong further convinced Sadat that Moscow preferred détente with the United States to full support of him against Israel. Instead, the Soviets constantly counselled him not to attack the Israelis and to have nothing to do with Americans. Therefore, he concluded, he could only get the Israelis out of the Sinai by getting the Americans to push them out. But his closeness to the Soviets only drove the Americans more into the hands of the Israelis. After he failed to persuade Washington to pressure Israel and after expelling the Soviet military in August 1972, he attacked Israeli-occupied territory to convince Washington of his seriousness. Sixth, Sadat's rapprochement with Saudi Arabia, one of his key moves in foreign policy, brought him not only money, but also a Saudi commitment to use the oil weapon against the West when Sadat attacked Israeli forces, putting yet more pressure on Washington to force Israel back to its 1967 boundaries. Seventh, he was apparently convinced that the Soviets had been behind the attempts of his opponents, Ali Sabry, Goma'a, and Sharaf, to remove him from power, which he forestalled by jailing them first. Moreover, he probably also believed the reports[2] that Sharaf, one of Nasser's intelligence chiefs, had been a controlled Soviet KGB agent since 1959. And, he had been made even more suspicious by Soviet pressure on him to support the pro-Communist coup against President Nimeiry of the Sudan. Instead, he aided Nimeiry. Eighth and finally,

[2]John Barron, *KGB* (New York: Reader's Digest Press, 1974), pp. 51-53, 58.

Sadat knew that turning against the Soviets would improve his position with most of the other Arabs, and he needed as much Arab support as possible to fight Israel. Recent Soviet support of Libya only strengthened Sadat's anti-Sovietism—with Qhadhdhafi as a friend, Moscow needs no enemy. It thus becomes clear why Sadat disengaged himself from the Soviets, fought the 1973 war, and since then has been betting on the new American policy of active even handed mediation.[3]

Syria has reason to be less suspicious of the Soviets than Sadat. Egypt and Iraq are potentially, if not always actually, the two strongest Arab powers. Syria, a secondary power, has historically been threatened by both. The Ba'ath leadership in Damascus has combined Arab nationalism with the Leninist organizational model. It is more conspiratorial, ideologically leftist, and clannish (it is overwhelmingly from the minority Alouite Muslim sect) than Egypt's post-Nasser leadership initially was. Unlike the situation in Cairo, the Damascus leadership has apparently never been penetrated by the Soviets. Syria is the more directly menaced by Israel, which bombed it severely during the 1973 war. It has been more sympathetic to a socialist economic model. It is less confident than Sadat that the United States will push the Israelis back, and it knows that Israel is much more determined to hold onto the Golan Heights than to the Sinai. Since 1970 President Hafaz Assad has moderated Syrian domestic and foreign policies. He is less pro-Soviet than his predecessor Jedid. He is importing Western civilian technology. His domestic policies are more moderate. He would probably like to diversify his now exclusively Soviet arms supplies by buying Western arms. Syria has been attempting to mediate a settlement of the recurrent Lebanese civil strife.[4] Assad has said, and probably means it, that he would sign a peace treaty with Israel once it goes back to the 1967 borders. His relations with the Iraqi Ba'ath leadership are now very strained, largely over the organizational issue of who will dominate the Ba'ath. His relations with Egypt are not nearly as good as in 1973, for he is very dissatisfied with the August

[3]See the analyses by A. H. [Arnold Hottinger] from Cairo in the *Neue Zürcher Zeitung*, July 1, 2, 12-13, 1975, and the two key documents for Soviet-Egyptian relations; Sadat's interviews with *As-Sivasah* (Kuweit), in MENA in Arabic, September 8, 1975, 1500 GMT (FBIS/MEA/9 September 1975/D1-13), and 22 August 1975/D3-12.) In my view, the best analysis of Soviet-Egyptian relations is Malcolm H. Kerr, "Soviet Influence in Egypt, 1967-73" in Alvin Z. Rubenstein, ed., *Soviet and Chinese Influence in the Third World* (New York: Praeger, 1975), pp. 88-108.

[4]*Ibid.*, June 10, 13, 25, July 7, 1975; Eric Rouleau, "Le Liban dans la guerre civile," *Le Monde*, 20 September 1975 *et seq.*

1975 Israeli-Egyptian disengagement agreement. But, he seems unlikely to break completely with Sadat, and his recent rapprochement with Jordan,[5] intended to reassure him against his fear of Egyptian desertion vis-à-vis Israel, and against Iraqi hostility, must concern the Soviets. The 2,500 or so Soviet military advisers in Syria are training Syrian troops in the use of Soviet weapons. There never have been any Soviet bases in Syria, and Syria has consistently refused to sign a friendship treaty with Moscow of the kind that Sadat and the Iraqis did. The Soviets have more influence in Damascus than any other foreign power, but they do not have domination or control, and Western technological presence in Syria is increasing rapidly. Generally, the Syrians, for their reasons, carry out policies which the Soviets, often for other reasons, also favor.

Jordan has rapidly overcome the isolation to which the Rabat Arab summit meeting seemed to have consigned it. King Hussein shared Syria's concern lest Egypt go too far with Israel. More importantly, he wanted to resume his favored international role as a stabilizing factor in the Middle East. His rapprochement with Syria furthered this aim and also worked against Soviet influence there, another of his goals. His threat to turn to the Soviets for missiles when the U.S. Congress initially cut his request from fourteen to six missile batteries persuaded Congress to reverse itself. (The U.S. Jewish-American lobby, not Israel, sparked the Congressional move.) Israel then did not object, for it pushed Washington to resume arms shipments to Israel. After the second Israeli-Egyptian disengagement agreement this consideration no longer applied and Israel therefore had no interest to have Soviet rather than U.S. missiles in Jordan. The whole episode strengthened Hussein's position and did not help the Soviets.

The reported decline of Soviet influence in Iraq is so recent that one must still reserve any final judgment on its extent and causes. Moscow acquired major influence in Baghdad because Iraq needed Soviet arms against Iran, U.S.-supported Saudi Arabia, and the Arab Gulf states, whose subversion Iraq supported. The Iraqi Ba'ath was ideologically anti-Capitalist, elitist, anti-Western, and "Arab Socialist"—but also anti-Communist. Because Baghdad was so anti-Iranian and anti-Saudi, it could not hope for American arms aid.

Eight developments seem to have contributed to Moscow's defeat in

<hr />

5A.H. [Arnold Hottinger] from Amman, "Jordanians Annäherung an seine arabischen Nachbarn," *Neue Zürcher Zeitung*, 19 June 1975; interview with King Hussein in *Al-Hawadith*, 10 July 1975 (FBIS/MEA/11 July 1975/F1-8.)

Iraq. First, the Ba'ath had always been ideologically opposed to Communism. Second, Baghdad's nationalization of the oil companies meant that it could sell its oil for hard currency in the West instead of bartering it for Soviet arms. Third, Baghdad resented Soviet resale, at higher prices, of its oil during and after the 1973 war. Fourth, the 1973 quadrupling of the price of oil gave it much more money. Fifth, Baghdad also resented Soviet opposition to its attempt in 1974, to crush the Kurdish rebellion. Sixth, the March 1975 Iraqi-Iranian rapprochement which ended the Kurdish rebellion, and their dispute over the Shatt al-Arab, freed Baghdad from the security menace from Tehran. Seventh, Baghdad was being wooed by Sadat and was increasingly concerned about its isolation in the Arab world. Finally, Baghdad rejected the Soviet desire to have it accept the existence of Israel and to deemphasize its support of Arab nationalism.[6]

Although Saudi Arabia's post-Faisal ladership has indicated some desire to normalize relations with the Soviet Union, this is not likely to change its fundamentally anti-Soviet policy. Its more active and flexible foreign policy, notably vis-à-vis Iran, is likely to be more effective than Faisal's was in countering the remaining Soviet influence in the Middle East.[7]

The *de facto* Iraqi leader, Sadam Hussein al-Takriti, played a major role in the Iraqi decision to come to terms with the Shah and devalue the Soviet connection. Iraq recently has been importing Western, and especially American, technology on a massive scale. It has normalized its relations with Iran and the Arab states. It has, probably, largely ceased its support of radical Arab subversive movements such as those in Dhofar which works against Iran and the Arab Gulf states· Its current support of the Shah's "Gulf Security Pact" would deprive Moscow of naval facilities in Iraq. It still is a leading member of the "front of rejection," i.e. opposed to any settlement with Israel. But this position is more rhetorical than real, since Iraq will not participate very actively in a future Arab-Israeli war any more than it has in the past. In sum, Iraq is thus returning to a policy of Arab non-alignment.

[6]See the essential analyses by A.H. [Arnold Hottinger] from Baghdad in the *Neue Zürcher Zeitung*, June 14-15, 17, 18, 1975, and, regarding the Kurdish problem, from Erbil in *Ibid.*, 10 June 1975 and from Suleimaniye, *ibid.*, 26 June 1975; his "Kurdistan After the Revolt," *Swiss Review of World Affairs*, July 1975, pp. 13-14; Ian Seymour, "Iraqi Oil Policy in Focus," *Middle Eastern Economic Survey*, vol. 18, no. 30 (June 20, 1975), supplement, pp. 1-5; and Smolansky, *The Soviet Union and the Middle East*, (Lewisburg, Pa., Bucknell University Press, 1974).

[7]"Saudi Arabia: Overture to the East," *Middle Eastern Economic Survey*, vol. 18, no. 38 (July 11, 1975), pp. 1-3; regarding Saudi-Iranian relations, see *Ibid.*, p. 4; Radio Moscow in Arabic, 8 July 1975, 1700 GMT (FBIS/SOV/10 July 1975/F3-4).

Since it no longer needs to be so dependent on Moscow, it can afford to pursue this talk. It is likely to continue this policy.

Even the PLO (Palestine Liberation Organization) is less opposed to an Arab-Israeli settlement, and less pro-Soviet, than most Westerners and almost all Israelis think. For the majority of the PLO, led by Arafat, radical rhetoric now conceals reluctant willingness to settle for the 1967 boundaries. This does not mean that the Palestinians will recognize the existence of Israel in their hearts, or stop hoping some time, some way, to destroy it. But, it does mean that most of them would now rather accept the 1967 borders and a Palestine state than remain homeless refugees, waiting for better days. It is also true that after such a settlement Arafat would be somewhat like de Valera, and Habbash akin to the Irish Republican Army (IRA), in the new Palestinian state. It is unlikely that Arafat and most Palestinians would then be pro-Soviet. On the contrary, for the same reasons as Sadat, including their need for Arab oil money, the Palestinians would move away from the Russians. Although the Soviets have been urging the PLO to accept a settlement, Moscow would quite likely, after such a settlement covertly aid the "Palestinian IRA." But the majority of the PLO leaders and the Soviets, now prefer a settlement on the 1967 boundaries. Even so, those boundaries would have to be guaranteed, not only by an international presence, but also by an American one in order to deter the Palestinian and radical Arabs from attempting to cross them.

Another major reason for the decline of Soviet power in the Middle East has been the rising power of Iran, and its rapprochement with Egypt and Saudi Arabia.[8] While the Shah has long since normalized relations with Moscow, his major security concern, like that of any strong Iranian government, remains the traditional Russian threat from the north. This explains his massive military buildup and his close relationship with the United States, which has the three requirements to be Iran's principal ally: it is powerful, far away, and anti-Soviet. The Shah's guarantee of the independence and security of Pakistan, and his rapprochement with India (in which, for India's not threatening Pakistan, India gets Iranian oil and credits) limit Soviet gains from its alliance with New Delhi. His rapprochement with China must infuriate Moscow. Finally, the new *de facto* ruler of Saudi Arabia, Crown Prince Fahd, has established much closer personal relations with the Shah

---

[8]Rouhollah K. Ramazani, "Emerging Patterns of Regional Relations in Iranian Foreign Policy," *Orbis*, vol. 18, no. 4 (Winter 1974), pp. 1043-1070; Marvin G. Weinbaum, "Iran and Israel: The Discreet Entente," *Ibid.*, pp. 1070-1087.

than King Faisal had, so that the Soviets cannot hope for much profit from any Iranian-Saudi disunity. Moscow's continued arms support, via Aden, of the faltering Dhofar rebellion against the Sultan of Oman, against which Iranian troops and the Iranian-Iraqi rapprochement have helped to turn the tide,[9] has further confirmed the Shah's inveterate suspicions of Moscow.

Finally, the curious episode of the Somali invitation, first of U.S. journalists and then of Senators and Congressmen, to visit the Somali port of Berbera, in order to demonstrate that the Soviets did not have a naval base there. This, after the Pentagon had released satellite photographs which, it alleged, proved that there was such a base, boomeranged against the Soviets. The Somalis refused to show the visitors exactly those installations which, according to the Pentagon's interpretation of the photographs, were Soviet servicing installations. Thereupon, the U.S. Congress passed the disputed appropriation for expanding the U.S. naval installation on the Indian Ocean island of Diego Garcia. Thus, the Soviets suffered another defeat, for the Diego Garcia naval facility will considerably strengthen the U.S. naval position in the Indian Ocean, and, therefore, in the Persian Gulf and the Red Sea. Moreover, the whole episode showed that Somali and even the People's Democratic Republic of Yemen are not necessarily reliable Soviet allies.[10]

In Israel, Rabin's government, in contrast to that of his predecessor, Golda Meir, has apparently abandoned the earlier Israeli view that Soviet influence in the Arab world, as long as it did not immediately menace Israel mili-

[9]See the most recent long analysis from Oman, by Thankmar Freiherr von Münchhausen in the *Frankfurter Allgemeine Zeitung*, 21 June 1975. See also the extracts from a captured PFLO document, indicating their defeats, in *Al-Nahar*, 10 June 1975, summarized in *Afro-Asian Affairs* (London), no. 13, (16 July 1975), p. 3.

[10]Sd. from Berbera in the *Neue Zürcher Zeitung*, 1 July 1975; Dennis Mullin from Berbera in *U.S. News and World Report*, 21 July 1975, pp. 31-32; meeting between Major General Said Barre, Chairman of Somali Revolutionary Council, and Senator Dewey Bartlett et al., in Radio Mogadiscio in Somali, 5 July 1975, 1700 GMT (FBIS/SAF/7 July 1975/B4); interview with Said Barre in *Al-Nahar*, 6 July 1975 (JPRS 65372, 1 August 1975, pp. 43-47); *Facts on File*, vol. 35, no. 1809 (12 July 1975), pp. 501-2; *Congressional Quarterly*, 2 August 1975 p. 1718. For Somali rapprochement with Saudi Arabia, see the Somali-Saudi communiqué regarding the Red Sea being "devoid of foreign forces," Radio Riyadh in Arabic, 6 May 1975, 1100 GMT (FBIS/MEA/7 May 1975/C3.) On the Indian Ocean, see S.P. Seth, "The Indian Ocean and Indo-American Relations," *Asian Survey*, vol. 15, no. 8 (August 1975), pp. 645-655; Alexander O. Ghebhardt, "Soviet and U.S. Interests in the Indian Ocean," *ibid.*, pp. 672-683; K.P. Misra, "International Politics in the Indian Ocean," *Orbis*, vol. 18, no. 4 (Winter 1975), pp. 1088-1108; Alvin J. Cottrell and R.M. Burrell, "Soviet-U.S. Naval Competition in the Indian Ocean," *Ibid.*, pp. 1109-1128. I also benefited from a paper by Shahram Chubin at the IISS Annual Meeting at Ronneby, Sweden, September 11-13, 1975, which will be published in the *Adelphi Papers*.

tarily, was in Israel's interest because it bound the United States closer to Israel and separated it from the pro-Soviet Arab states. He has also tried to split Egypt from the other Arab states but has been unwilling, in part because of domestic pressures, to carry out this policy to its logical conclusions by making generous concessions to Sadat. Moreover, he has overestimated his possibilities in this respect. Sadat cannot make a separate peace with Israel (i.e., abandon Syria, Jordan, and the Palestinians) without losing his financial support from Saudi Arabia and Kuwait, losing his leading role in the Arab world. And he would have to back all the Egyptian territory occupied by Israel. But Rabin will not, and indeed for domestic political reasons cannot, now evacuate all the Israeli-occupied territory, or agree to a Palestinian state on the West Bank. Jordan, no longer weak and isolated, cannot accept, in a disengagement agreement, the maintenance of the Israeli paramilitary settlements along the Jordan River. Indeed, in the future the question, for Jerusalem, of evacuating any of the settlements on the Golan Heights or along the Jordan is likely to be a more difficult one in domestic politics, and therefore a more unlikely decision for the Israeli government to take, than evacuation of some of what it considers strategically necessary territory. Thus, Rabin's policy, although more flexible than Golda Meir's, still remains one of gaining time. Therefore the Soviets and the Arab radicals can hope that U.S. mediation efforts will eventually fail, and that Soviet influence and Arab radicalism will again return to the Arab East. Thus, although Israel's agreement to the second disengagement agreement with Egypt contributed to the decline of Soviet influence in the Middle East, its refusal to evacuate the occupied territories strengthens Soviet hopes to recover their lost influence in the Middle East.

Do the Soviets want a Middle Eastern settlement on the 1967 boundaries? It has long been the conventional wisdom that Moscow wants neither peace nor war in the Middle East, since war might wreck détente with the United States and peace would end the Arabs' need for Soviet arms and therefore, Soviet influence. I do not think that this is still the case. The Soviets now give greater priority to East-West détente. The Arabs are getting out from under Soviet arms aid anyway. Even after a settlement they will not want to be completely dependent on Western arms, so they will want some continuing relationship with Moscow. Finally, if Egypt, Saudi Arabia, Syria, and Jordan decide to accept a settlement with Israel, Moscow cannot prevent it.[11]

[11]Amnon Kapeliouk, *Israël: la fin des mythes* (Paris: Albin Michel, 1975); Yair

I therefore do not agree, except in a public relations sense, with the view increasingly heard in the West, that the United States should "get the Soviets in on a Middle Eastern settlement." The U.S. has, it is true, no interest in barring them from it completely, if only because of Arab insistence on Soviet participation so as not to become totally dependent on Washington. We must cooperate with the Soviets in limiting and managing any new military crisis there, and we have an interest in deterring them from taking too much advantage of future opportunities if our mediation breaks down. But, why should we be more pro-Soviet than Sadat, or the Shah? We have aided, and profited from, the Arab limitation of Soviet influence in the Middle East. We and the Soviets are, and will remain, competitors there. The Soviets cannot decisively help us to get a settlement—only the Arabs and Israelis can do that. We should continue to do what we have been doing: cautiously and without publicity continue to cooperate with Arabs, Israelis, and the Shah to lower Soviet influence in the Middle East.

THE SECOND ISRAELI-EGYPTIAN DISENGAGEMENT AGREEMENT

The August 1975 (second) disengagement agreement between Egypt and Israel was, in my view, one of Kissinger's greatest achievements, and a major move away from war. It was also a further blow to the Soviet position in the Middle East. For the first time, Egypt and Israel renounced the use of force for at least three years, deescalated their economic and propaganda war, and established a mixed commission to work out the details of the agreement. The United States established a minimal ground presence of civilian electronic technicians in the Sinai whose removal Egypt and Israel agreed not to demand unilaterally, and promised massive economic aid to both sides, thus further defusing the East-West aspects of the conflict.[12] At the least,

Evron, "Israelische Aussenpolitik nach dem Yom-Kippur-Krieg." Versuche und Versäumnisse auf der Suche nach Frieden," *Europa Archiv*, vol. 30, no. 11 (June 10, 1975), pp. 351-360. See also Martin van Creveld, *Military Lessons of the Yom Kippur War: Historical Perspective*. The Washington Papers, no. 24 Beverly Hills and London: Sage, 1975; Ammon Sella, "What Will the Next War Be Like?" Research Paper no. 13. The Hebrew University Soviet and East European Research Center, mimeo., June 1975; and Elizabeth Monroe and A.H. Farrar-Hockley, *The Arab-Israel War, October 1973. Background and Events.* Adelphi Paper no. 111 (London: IISS, Winter 1974/5.)

[12]See the excellent analyses by Eric Rouleau in *Le Monde*, 3 September 1975 and by William Beecher in *The Boston Sunday Globe*, 7 September 1975. See also "Russian Tea, Sympathy and Guns," *The Economist*, 13 September 1975, pp. 17-18,

the disengagement will postpone another war, during and after which the Soviets might at least for a time regain some of their lost influence. It rebuilt, somewhat the present Administration's credibility in the eyes of the Arabs, which had been shaken by its initial inability to carry Congress along on the Turkish arms embargo and Jordanian missile issues. Washington's withholding of military and economic aid to Israel until the disengagement was signed was the major factor in Israel's agreeing to sign it. The agreement opened the way to a second round of Israeli-Syrian disengagement negotiations, which will be much more difficult to conclude successfully on the Egyptian talks but which will, if they succeed, probably lower somewhat Soviet influence in Damascus, and gain more time to prevent another war. In any case, the agreement strengthened Sadat's domestic position, made him even more anti-Soviet, and justified his further betting on the American card.

Because only an evaluation of the agreement can enable one to judge its meaning for Moscow, and because it has become a subject of considerable controversy in the United States, the agreement requires detailed analysis. I shall, therefore, set forth what are in my view, its positive and negative points for the four states most involved; Israel, Egypt, the United States, and the Soviet Union.

For Israel the agreement was, on balance, positive. Through Egypt's renunciation of the use of force, Jerusalem has gained a very good chance for peace for at least three years, and perhaps an important step toward eventual Israeli-Egyptian direct negotiations. The agreement greatly improved Israel's relations with the United States, which had been worsened by the March 1975 breakdown of the negotiations. This will result in massive U.S. economic and military aid. The military aid may well include such advanced weapons systems as the Pershing missile, whose longer range, with conventional warheads, will improve Israeli deterrence against the Arabs' Soviet-made SCUD missiles, and whose nuclear warhead capability will psychologically compensate Israel for the threat of eventual Arab quantitative arms superiority. The United States has assured Israel of enough petroleum supply to make up for the return of the Abu Rudeis oil field to Egypt. The presence

---

with whose view that "Russia is probably stronger in the Middle East today than it was before the signing of the Sinai accord" I do not agree. The initially published texts of the agreements are in *The New York Times*, 2 September 1975, and texts and/or summaries of subsequent published parts of the agreements in *The New York Times*, 10, 12, 18 September 1975. Or Ford with regarding to military aid to Egypt, see his interview with *The Los Angeles Times*, 2 September 1975.

of U.S. civilian electronic technicians on the new Sinai disengagement line makes another Egyptian attack much less likely. The agreement is likely to lead to the return of many more Egyptians to the Suez Canal area, which will also work against any Egyptian resumption of hostilities. Egypt has agreed to allow Israel bound cargoes through the Suez Canal and to limit its anti-Israeli propaganda. (Indeed, at the recent Lima nonaligned foreign ministers meeting Egypt opposed the suspension of Israel from the UN General Assembly.) The United States has agreed not to negotiate with the PLO until it recognizes Israel's right to exist, to deter Soviet intervention against Israel, to prevent the withdrawal of the UN Emergency Force, and not to pressure Israel for any further disengagement agreements with Egypt or Jordan.

As for Israel's losses, Israeli critics of the agreement maintain that by surrendering the Mitla and Gidi passes, Israel's military situation has worsened. (Its supporters feel that this is outweighed by the Egyptian renunciation of force the U.S. arms supply, and U.S. civilian technicians on the new line.) The critics add that the agreement makes Israel more dependent on the United States, that Israel was forced by U.S. economic and military pressure to sign the agreement, and that the United States will soon force Israel, against its will, to open new disengagement negotiations with Syria, and thus, to continue pushing Israel back toward the 1967 boundaries. Other critics maintain that Israel has surrendered the demilitarization principle.[13]

Egypt also gained more than it lost from the agreement. It gained back territory which included the Gidi and Mitla passes and the Abu Rudeis oil fields ($300 million per year). It also gained Israeli renunciation of force, and the presence of U.S. civilian technicians, which make an Israeli preemptive strike much less likely. It will get U.S. economic aid and is now more likely to get Western investment. President Ford has indicated that he favors some military aid to Egypt. The prospect of at least three years of peace will make it much easier for Egypt to turn to the problems of its crisis-ridden domestic economy. The U.S. is committed to launching Israeli-Syrian disengagement negotiations. Egypt has thus insured continued movement, maintained its ties with Saudi Arabia, and eventually, because of Saudi and Kuweiti financial pressure, will probably again improve its ties with Syria and the PLO. On the debit side, in the short run Egypt's relations with Syria and the PLO have worsened.[14] Sadat has moved to an even more anti-Soviet position,

[13]Mattiyahu Peled in *Ma'ariv*, 15 August 1975 (FBIS/ME/28 August 1975/N6-9).

[14] Markham from Beirut in *The New York Times*, 2 September 1975.

which, one might argue, makes him even more dependent on the United States, which will not force Israel back to the 1967 boundaries, and he has thereby unwisely limited his freedom of maneuver. Finally, since the United States has assured Israel that the next Israeli-Egyptian negotiation will be about a peace treaty, no further disengagement agreements are possible.

The United States also gained. It has probably postponed war for at least three years, and thereby oil limitation, confrontation with the Soviet Union, and alliance crisis. It has encouraged the moderates in the Arab world, particularly Sadat, who is now more pro-American and anti-Soviet than ever.[15] It has further reduced Soviet influence in the area. In short, it has transformed what was primarily an East-West confrontation in the Middle East into a West-West one, between two allies of the United States, Israel and Egypt. On the debit side, the agreement will cost the United States up to $3 billion in the first year, and perhaps $8-10 billion within a 3-5 year period. It will escalate the arms race in the area, particularly if the United States gives Israel Pershing missiles, and may thereby make another war much more destructive. If new Israeli-Syrian disengagement negotiations drag on or fail, it may either freeze the status quo for a long period and thereby work against an overall settlement or, alternatively, if Israeli-Syrian negotiations break down, the Israeli-Egyptian agreement may also prematurely collapse and war ensue. The agreement may split the Arab world and thus enable the Soviets to gain more influence with Syria, the PLO, and the radical Arab states. Finally, the placing of American civilian technicians in the Sinai, dangerously involves the United States in an explosive situation. If, it is argued, the U.S. does pull them out in a rising crisis situation, it will fatally tempt either Israel or Egypt to launch a preemptive attack. And, if it does not, they may be in such danger of being overrun during such an attack that Washington will be faced with the choice of sacrificing them or intervening militarily to evacuate them. The agreement's proponents reply that there can be neither permanent or even temporary peace in the Middle East without some U.S. ground presence, and that the risks of this, like the financial costs to the United States, are far outweighed by the risks and costs of an otherwise inevitable war and oil limitation. Also, they continue, the argument that the agreement tends to freeze the status quo and thus blocks an overall settlement incorrectly assumes that the United States can, in terms of its own domestic politics, force Israel to such a settlement; a settle-

[15]See footnote 3, supra.

ment which would have to involve near-total Israeli evacuation of the occupied territories. Thus the better, an overall settlement, which is now impossible, is the enemy of the good, the disengagement agreement, which at least postpones another war.[16]

The Soviets are the losers in the short run. Egypt, where they invested so much, has effectively broken with them. The United States is for the present the only effective mediator in the area and, is therefore, close to being the arbiter of the situation. The Geneva Conference, where the Soviets are a cochairman, is farther off than ever. Western technology, credits, and arms will now flood into the Arab world. The level of Soviet influence there is now so low that while the United States continues to give lip-service to Soviet involvement, it may, in fact, exclude it, and neither the United States nor most of the Arabs see any reason to bring Moscow back in. On the credit side, Moscow has temporarily found some new opportunities with the Syrians and with the PLO, although Saudi and Kuweiti money may well counteract it again. And Moscow, as we shall see below, can hope that American success and Soviet failure is temporary.

In my view the positive aspects of the agreement far outweigh the negative ones for Israel, Egypt, and the United States, while the negative ones far outweigh the positive ones for the Soviet Union. Why, then, did the Soviets not try harder to prevent the agreement? They certainly had ample reason to do so. Despite their overall priority for détente with the United States, they knew that the agreement would further worsen their position and improve Washington's. But, they had little or no alternative because what they had been advocating, the reconvening of the Geneva Conference, was no longer credible to most of the Arabs, who knew it would get nowhere. On the other hand, Moscow probably calculated that Kissinger would find the next disengagement negotiations, close between Israel and Syria, much more difficult to conclude, and subsequent ones even more so. Moscow therefore could hope that eventually Kissinger's "small steps" policy will come up against a stone wall and the Arabs would have no alternative but to return to Geneva. By then, they could also hope, they will have greatly improved their relations with the Palestinians and reestablished diplomatic relation with Israel.[17]

[16]Leslie H. Gelb, "Washington's Own Battle of the Sinai," *The New York Times*, 21 September 1975, IV, p. 2.

[17]See the penetration analysis by Avigdor Livni from Jerusalem in *Corriere della Sera*, 3 September 1975.

THE FUTURE

Soviet blunders, technological backwardness, higher oil prices, and the post-1972 shift in American policy have been the main factors in Moscow's precipitous loss of influence in the Middle East. Can and will the Soviets recoup their losses? They cannot overcome the conservative Arabs' oil wealth, nor can they keep from making yet more blunders or overcome their technological backwardness. But, Russian history, Soviet ideology, the massive Soviet arms investment in the area, continued competition with the United States and China, the probability of recurrent intra-Arab dissension, and the Soviet ruling elite's sense of history, (which takes into account rising Soviet military power and recurring Arab radicalism) all indicate that the Russians will try to regain their influence in the area.

It is a future failure of American Middle Eastern policy on which the Soviets count, with considerable reason, and for which they are waiting, with outward equanimity but inward impatience. One should not be deluded by the second Egyptian-Israeli disengagement agreement into thinking the U.S. diplomatic successes guarantee that Soviet defeats in the Middle East are likely to continue. Perhaps renewed Israeli-Syrian negotiations will succeed, perhaps not. Perhaps Secretary Kissinger's most recent alternative proposal[18] for an informal multilateral meeting of the parties instead of or in addition to the Geneva Conference, in order to postpone the PLO issue, could gain time. But, sooner or later, the moment of truth will come. At some point, whether on the Golan Heights, the West Bank, or East Jerusalem, Arab-Israeli negotiations will break down irreparably unless Washington brings irresistible pressure to bear on them, and especially on Israel, to compromise. This will be all the more difficult after the delivery of massive military and economic aid which the United States made to Israel to get it to sign the disengagement agreement. The Arabs, increasingly confident of their power, pushed forward by the revival of Islam, and looking forward to their reemergence as a world force after centuries of Ottoman and Western humiliation, will accept nothing less than complete Israeli withdrawal to the 1967 frontiers. But, no elected Israeli government in the foreseeable future can accept this, unless, it can convince its people, as Ben Gurion did in 1957, that it must yield to irresistible U.S. pressure.

Such irresistible American pressure is possible but unlikely. If a Democratic President is elected in 1976, U.S. policy is likely to become more pro-

[18]*The New York Times*, 23 September 1975.

Israeli. Even if President Ford is reelected, there will still be a pro-Israeli Democratic majority in Congress. The Arabs, who historically prefer the glory of courage to the shame of compromise, will probably also make blunders, such as trying to get Israel suspended from the UN General Assembly, which may well reverse their recent gains in U.S. public opinion. The eventual result will be yet another war, another oil limitation, another NATO crisis, the isolation of the United States and Israel, and a temporary Soviet recouping of much of its recent losses in the Middle East. The Egyptians and the Syrians will have to have Soviet arms during and after what will probably be an overwhelming Israeli victory. Even so the Arabs will still confront the fact that only the United States, and not the Soviet Union, will then be able to get the Israelis out of the territories they will again conquer. And then, one must hope, the United States will finally give primacy to its vital national interest in a Middle Eastern settlement rather than domestic ethnic politics.

The darker the future prospects are, the more statesmen must try to prove them wrong. The most realistic objective for the United States in the Middle East remains the gaining of time; enough time to become less dependent on Arab oil; enough time to educate the American people to our true interests, and indeed to those of Israel and the Arabs; enough time to make a settlement before the spiral of war turns atomic; enough time to consolidate our own position in the Middle East, and thereby keep the Soviet position as weak as it is. And, finally, enough time to learn the folly of giving domestic ethnic politics priority over U.S. national interests. One must hope that we will have enough time to learn these lessons, and act accordingly, before another Middle Eastern war breaks out. Or will it take another war before we learn?

The Indian Subcontinent and the Indian Ocean: the Soviet Union as an Asian Power

Dieter Braun

The Indian Ocean and South Asia are, geographically, the farthest area in the world from the United States, both east- or west-bound (this has a natural bearing on Washington's policy orientation). It is closer to Europe. However, after the colonial era many of the stimuli to Europeans to engage themselves have vanished. It is not very distant from Asia's most populous country, China. But throughout history the Himalayas have proved to be a formidable barrier to closer contacts and mutual familiarization, and China has not yet developed a far-reaching maritime arm.

The USSR, by contrast, has both sustained and rationalized the 19th century Czarist southward drive. Moscow's policy towards the Indian Ocean and, in particular, towards South Asia is underpinned by geographical and ethnical proximity, historical continuity, and economic and strategic motivations. Since the reopening of the Suez Canal, the Soviet Union is the nearest sea power, and in addition, has easiest access by land.

The Sino-Soviet rift in the 1960s has caused a near-obsession on the part of the USSR to establish her credentials as an Asian power, entitled to partake in that continent's decision-making processes. Détente with the United States as well as Europe was a forceful promoter of an idea which found trine. The idea, Mr. Brezhnev's contribution to a new framework of regional policy, was called a "system of collective security in Asia." Dismissed too lightly in the West, in many Asian states as some Soviet trial balloon, and furiously attacked by China, it keeps on serving as a useful, if opaque, pattern for Soviet policy objectives in a part of the world where the Russians, whether China or the West approve or not, are present in their own right, and from where they cannot be wished away.

ADVANCES AND SETBACKS IN SOUTH ASIA

Afghanistan, the age-old crossroads of Asia, is the key area for any access by land from the Soviet Asian republics in the direction of the populous plains of the Indus and Ganges rivers. It is imperative for the USSR that this country be secured as a buffer against any southern approach and to prevent its slipping under potentially hostile influence. In this, Moscow has been fairly successful, particularly since Western interest in Afghanistan has, for a variety of reasons, shown a marked and steady decline. The coup d'état in July 1973 seemed to have further strengthened Soviet influence.

Recently, however, a new factor has entered regional policies. Iran, pro-Western and a member of CENTO, today has both the material means and the political will to "buy off" the Afghans, and to prevent them thereby from leaning too exclusively on Moscow. Still, being a very poor country with a 1200-mile border on Soviet Central Asia, Afghanistan has no real choice but to keeping friendly relations with the USSR. Its policy options are strictly limited, and this is well understood and respected by all of Afghanistan's neighbors and partners, China included. It is the case of Finland in Asia.

With a firm foothold in Afghanistan, the Russians have tried, for a long time and patiently, to convince the Pakistanis of the advantages of direct overland trade and traffic between the USSR, Iran, Afghanistan and the Indian subcontinent. Good roads exist, lacking railway links could be built, and raw materials and industrial goods exchanged to mutual benefit. There is some soundness in this for anybody who looks at the map from a viewpoint in Soviet Central Asia, and who thinks of future trade needs and patterns.

After Khrushchev's fall, the Soviet leaders shifted their policy in that direction. Pakistan received better treatment in spite of its membership in

CENTO and SEATO. Even Soviet arms shipments started in 1968, much to India's chagrin. In the spring of 1969, Mr. Kosygin seemed to be very close to the coveted goal of regional economic cooperation under Moscow's aegis, as an integral part of the collective security idea. Pakistan nearly consented, but then stepped back again. The time was not ripe.

It is a basic feature of overall Soviet policy that a line once taken up is not easily abandoned, even after a series of setbacks. This consistency is both a strength and weakness of its system. Thus, the "Kosygin Plan" of connecting Soviet Asia with the subcontinent by a network of communications and trade relations came up in a revised manner after the dismemberment of Pakistan, although this country was not in the mood to give the Soviets, who had been instrumental in the creation of Bangladesh, a free passage through its territory. However, a previous Soviet offer to build a steelmill near Karachi was accepted (March 1974). When Pakistan's Prime Minister Bhutto visited Moscow in October 1974, Mr. Kosygin, during a dinner speech, said: "After the metallurgical plant has gone into operation, prerequisites may arise for the expansion of Pakistan's trade with its closest neighbors—for example, those that possess iron ore and coal."[1] The example fits India and Afghanistan.

Accordingly, the USSR after 1971 has supported every move to straighten out the rather formidable rifts and differences between Pakistan, India and Bangladesh. Mr. Bhutto, in his answer to the above mentioned speech by Mr. Kosygin, expressly acknowledged such "positive influence" and "constructive contribution" for which Pakistan owed gratitude.[2] But, the Russians left no doubt that this process of normalization was regarded as the road to a subcontinental framework of peace in accordance with their collective security design. To be effective, the "system" needs as pivots leading regional powers which support it in their own national interest. In South Asia, the obvious choice was India; treaty-bound with the USSR and having emerged prominently from the restructuring of forces in that area.

Again, these schemes did not materialize due to unforeseen circumstances. The energy crisis, or rather, OPEC price policy from late 1973 onwards, shifted the economic priorities of all the oil importing countries. They feverishly tried to secure the least disadvantageous conditions for a basic necessity, oil and its derivatives. In this field, the USSR was in no position its first expression in 1969—synchronized, as it were, with the Nixon Doc-

[1]*Pravda*, 25 October 1975, p. 4.
[2]*Ibid.*

to compete with OPEC countries and, consequently, lost some leverage in regional policies to the West Asian oil producing states.

Consequently, India no longer denounced Iranian armament and hegemonic designs, but discovered much common ground of general policy orientation. Iran's enhanced influence in Afghanistan has been mentioned above. Pakistan and Bangladesh did not recognize each other, as Moscow and New Delhi had earlier hoped, through Indian mediation, but rather, in the name of Islamic brotherhood (Lahore summit). Altogether, the Soviet Union was very much left out of a process for which it was poorly equipped, both economically and ideologically.

Developments in Bangladesh were another setback to Soviet plans in South Asia. Even with Mujibur Rahman alive and firmly in power, relations had somewhat soured by 1973. His assassination and the events of the following months upset previous Soviet calculations. Hence, the very strong, negative reactions in Moscow, whereas in the West, there was quiet resignanation over Bangladesh's development under any regime, and China openly approved of the new situation.

To the USSR, Bangladesh, as created in December 1971, obviously held out shining promises. First, it was a symbol of the USSR's correct assessment of an Asian crisis situation, with a victorious outcome, in opposition to both the United States and China. Second, it proved the usefulness of a bilateral treaty relationship (with India, in August 1971) that had overtones of military guarantees without precisely saying so. Third, it opened up prospects of enlarging and securing the Indian sphere of influence; cf. the Indo-Bangladesh treaty of March 1972 which strictly followed the tenor of the Indo-Soviet one, thus offering an example to other regional states.

The new nation's (and that of its majority party's Awami League) avowed principles of socialism and secularism, further signified a break from traditional Western as well as Islamic orientation, showing instead distinct parallels to the Indian Congress Party. There were good prospects of participation of other "progressive" parties and groupings, if not in government, then in important decision-making processes. Thus, the groundwork for cooperation with the USSR was laid in the ideological field as well. Regarding foreign policy, there was another Asian state which subscribed to basic Soviet goals from the beginning (e.g. Mujibur Rahman's Moscow visit in March 1972 or the "Asian Peace Conference" at Dacca in May 1973). Additionally, Bangladesh seemed to have no choice but to follow the Indian lead, in view of its geographic location and economic dependency.

All of these previous Soviet assumptions were no longer valid after 15 August 1975. On the contrary, Bangladesh became a potential security risk for the USSR, in view of its strategic position on the Gulf of Bengal and its proximity to China. Soviet policy makers seemed to be deeply disturbed; the press issued ominous warnings. A week after Mujibur Rahman's assassination, *Pravda* registered "concern" that hostile forces—Maoism, imperialism, inner reaction—might gain the upper hand in Bangladesh, and that such a development would negatively affect the situation on the Indian subcontinent, regarded as one of the very important factors in international relations.[3] The reshuffling of forces in November 1975 which led to the physical elimination of the pro-Indian group of former political leaders, caused a further escalation. A *Pravda* commentary, entitled "The alarming situation in Bangladesh," underscored the Kremlin's concern that the Dacca government might swing into a full-fledged pro-Chinese and pro-Western course. "These forces should be rebuffed," *Pravda's* commentator wrote, otherwise the country would lose all the gains of the liberation struggle.[4]

It is improbable, though, that in view of strong geopolitical compulsions Bangladesh would head for a collision course with India; i.e. line up actively with China and with Pakistan in some anti-Indian grouping. There are certain rules of behavior vis-à-vis India for any government in Dacca. But the forces could shift considerably. China may take diplomatic and political positions in Dacca to counteract Indo-Soviet "domination" of the subcontinent (as perceived in Peking) as it is doing in other states adjacent to India. The sociopolitical ferment in Bangladesh as evidenced for instance in a soldiers' mutiny against some officers in November 1975, makes this country more receptive to Maoist ideas than any other South Asian state. But the strong Muslim mentality in Bangladesh imposes limits on the appeal of "instant revolution."

Bangladesh borders on areas that are in themselves politically unstable, and prone to violence and to various kinds of insurrection. There is West Bengal with its latent revolutionary potential; there are the Indian states bordering Burma with insurgency going on (Mizoram) or recently quelled (Nagaland) that are supported to a degree by China; there are the Burmese northern states, in open rebellion against the government in Rangoon, again with China's barely concealed hand stirring the pot.

[3]*Pravda*, 22 August 1975, see also *Izvestia*, 2 September 1975.
[4]*Pravda*, 23 November 1975, p. 5.

In a long-range strategic view, the area between the Chinese province of Yunnan and Bangladesh, offering the shortest geographical connection between China and the Indian Ocean, could be brought under control by Peking without insurmountable difficulties. The stake China might have for pursuing this objective could be to counter a Russian access by land to this ocean, possibly via Afghanistan and southwest Pakistan (Baluchistan)*. Today, both moves are speculation. In the short run, it is bad enough for Moscow that Bangladesh can hardly be considered a state within the Soviet sphere of influence or, for that matter, under safe Indian control.

THE MAIN PARTNER: INDIA

It has been repeated often that India is too big, too complex, and too independent-minded to ever become a Soviet satellite. This has blurred critical analysis. The notion of a satellite is certainly inappropriate for the India of today, but Indo-Soviet relations are, by any counting, special relations. The question arises: are these special relations one set among other international links, or are they the decisive set, according to which the others are adjusted? In answer, it is necessary to take a closer look at India's present view of its role in Asia and in the world.

Two main foreign policy objectives have remained constant in India in recent years: (1) to be a power "in its own right" vis-à-vis the major and, in particular, the superpowers, (i.e. to be no longer an object of their mutual global dealings, détente or no détente); and (2) to be recognized by all countries concerned as the prominent, preeminent major power in the South Asian subregion, from Afghanistan to Bangladesh, and from Nepal to Sri Lanka. Both objectives are connected with regional and international policies in the Indian Ocean area.

It is India's dilemma that these aims have little chance of being achieved, given the very slow growth or, rather, the near-stagnation of the Indian economy. Thus, India remains dependent on both superpowers for economic and military aid, and it is not being taken seriously by its neighbors as the major regional power, due to its lack of economic strength. Realization of

* There are widespread reports that the USSR is supporting the "Greater Baluchistan" movement and may have an interest in the "Pakhtunistan" issue.

⁵The President of the Congress Party, Borooah, said recently: "—until our economic power improves, agricultural production increases and industrial production progresses, our power cannot escalate. In this world, only the powerful command respect." *Times of India,* 27 December 1975, p. 1.

this basic insufficiency[5] has led to frustration in India, and, consequently, to various means of compensation. Anti-Western attacks are part of them.[6] Others are indigenous advances in sophisticated technological fields, particularly in nuclear and space science.

To develop, in spite of these impediments, the appearance of power wherever it is feasible, seems to be an irresistible urge for India's leaders. However, there is also a strong element of "Realpolitik" involved; India's threat perceptions and security interests must be taken into account. Hence, India's armed forces are designed to provide outward as well as domestic security. The USSR has increasingly, and in some areas exclusively, come to the fore to help India achieve a high degree of defense preparedness and military muscle. Indeed, "the centrality of military and strategic factors in Indo-Soviet relations"[7] should be the basis of any assessment of the present and future link between Moscow and Delhi.

THE SOVIET UNION, INDIA, AND CHINA: ANOTHER ASIAN TRIANGLE

Given the Soviet Union's wariness of an extension of Chinese influence in Asia by land, and of American power by sea, the strategic location of the Indian subcontinent, and particularly the landmass of India itself, is obvious. Indian troops face the Chinese near the crest of the Himalayas from Kashmir in the west to the Burmese border in the east. They are now incomparably better positioned, trained, and equipped than in October/November 1962 when the Chinese were able to overrun them in many parts of that border area. This improvement is to a large extent due to Soviet military aid within the last decade.

India has its problem of unsettled frontiers with China, just like the USSR. Thus, Peking's cool attitude towards New Delhi must be as reassuring to Moscow as the Sino-Soviet conflict is to India, since it makes dependence mutual. The USSR benefits greatly from India's mistrust in everything Chinese, whereas India, being the weak and junior partner of the Russian superpower, can derive a sense of basic security from this constellation. Any rapprochement between the two Communist giants would certainly decrease India's value to the USSR.

[6]For a recent example see the speeches of Mrs. Gandhi during the All India Congress Party session in December 1975.

[7]M.F. Franda, "India and the Soviets," *American Universities Field Staff, South Asia Series,* June 1975, p. 1.

China makes it quite clear that it regards India as being not much more than a stooge of Soviet social imperialism. It sees no advantage in befriending India in the context of its overall Asia policy. This holds true in spite of the exchange of ambassadors in 1976. One might also speculate that China is deliberately driving India into a greater dependence on the USSR to let it repeat Peking's own experience with the Russians during the fifties. This feature has repeatedly come up in Chinese statements on Indo-Soviet relations. Whatever the reasons, it would seem that in the foreseeable future there is not much hope of restoring more than an appearance of normalcy between the two largest Asian nations.

In view of the above, India remains dependent on the USSR for strategic reasons. Between China and India, however comparable they may be in an Asian context by their size, population, and industrial potential, a basic asymmetry exists insofar as China is a nuclear-weapon power and India is not. Given the state of U.S. relations with both India and China, it is very unlikely, from the New Delhi view, that the United States would come to its rescue in case of Chinese nuclear threat or blackmail. Although there is no published security pact between India and the USSR to cover such an ventuality, it is a fair assumption that Soviet interests in the area would deter any such nuclear challenge that might arise from Peking.

To Indian defense planners, this situation is certainly not ideal for a future containing many uncertainties. Consequently, they have tried for a number of years to develop their own indigenous defense capacity, including highly sophisticated weaponry. Within the Third World, India possesses the most advanced arms production program. The aim of these costly efforts, which have raised surprisingly little criticism within India itself, is independence from outside suppliers including the USSR. However, while this is still unachieved, India will have to depend even more on Russian arms deliveries, transfer of technology, and favorable credit conditions to finance its own arms self-sufficiency.[8]

Even with conventional armament sufficiency assured, India will be unable to match China as long as it does not possess at least a rudimentary nuclear force as a deterrent. The "peaceful" explosion in the Rajasthan desert in May 1974 has indicated that the Indian nuclear option will be kept

[8]SIPRI; "The Arms Trade with the Third World," 1971–75; Stockholm. H. Wulf, *"Indien: Militarisierung und der Aufbau einer autonomen Rüstungsproduktion,"* *Internationales Asien-Forum,* Juli 1975, p. 272-301; S.P. Cohen, "Security Issues in South Asia," *Asian Survey,* March 1975, pp. 202-14.

open. The USSR has studiously avoided condemnation or even undue discussion on, this event which, according to official announcements in New Delhi, is to be followed by others. It looks as if the Soviets, in spite of their "principled stand" on nonproliferation, are prepared to accept a nuclear-weapon equipped India in the higher interest of their Asia policy, and as an additional counterweight to China. However, such a development is not around the corner when one considers the performance of Indian industry in the nuclear, space, and electronic sectors.

The situation is not without its paradoxical aspects. China accuses India of dependence on the USSR, and India is conscious of its strategic dependence, vis-à-vis Chinese nuclear missiles. Thus, India is trying to develop an indigenous capacity in order to steer clear of (official or unofficial) Soviet security guarantees, and, while following this course, India obviously has no choice but to become ever more dependent on Soviet support, both technological and diplomatic. Thus, China, by its intransigence towards Indian feelers for a genuine rapprochement, causes India to get ever more enmeshed in the Soviet imperialist net.

INDIAN OCEAN POLICY: SOVIET AND INDIAN MOTIVATIONS

The other front for the USSR is the Indian Ocean; the antagonist there being the United States. There, India occupies some important positions. Its north-western coast is very close to the Persian Gulf area. Further south, a future Indian navy might gain control over sea lanes leading in and out of the Gulf in the direction of the Pacific (by then, the Maldives should be effectively included in India's security perimeter). Towards South East Asia, India possesses the Andaman and Nicobar islands, close to Burma, Malaysia, and Indonesia (Sumatra). India's northeastern coast forms part of the Gulf of Bengal.

The 1971 Indo-Pakistan war has convinced Indian strategists of the importance of naval power. India's aim of achieving the preeminent position in its subregion can hardly be pursued without naval predominance. Iran's efforts in this respect did not fail to have a strong impact on India, because Iran, in spite of much improved bilateral relations, is a potential future rival in South West Asia, where it has aligned with Pakistan and the CENTO pact. Growing superpower rivalry in the Indian Ocean, particularly since

October 1973, has heightened India's awareness of its maritime importance. New Delhi's strong support of the littoral states' Peace Zone proposal must be seen in the context of its own national and regional ambitions. Should the superpowers be obliged to withdraw militarily from the Indian Ocean, India would stand out conspicuously as one of the few leading littoral powers.

With these premises of nationalist goals, it is not immediately evident to western observers why Indian and Soviet policies regarding the Indian Ocean should appear to converge. In fact, this appearance is inaccurate, although not altogether wrong. Some explanation is provided by recent history.

1971 was an important year for the Indian subcontinent. Bangladesh was born under much painful laboring. The United States contributed by dispatching the spectacular "Enterprise" task force; sent to the Gulf of Bengal during the armed hostilities. This event had a strong impact on India. Up to the present day it has added to the Indian's threat perception, and it has lead to a psychological acceptance of a Soviet shield against its recurrence. The USSR has, understandably, made the most of this windfall. But, before this and after, it has done much more to earn Indian sympathies.

Consistent Soviet support for India over the last twenty years in many fields, particularly in fields of prime national interest (Kashmir, Bangladesh, public sector industry, oil exploration, and arms) has created a general climate of trust to the USSR; a rare achievement for Moscow in its international relations anywhere and most of all in Asia. Indira Gandhi has many times given public expression thereto.[9] At the same time, U.S. policy towards Asia in general, and the subcontinent in particular, has held little attraction to India. In spite of more aid than the USSR and human exchanges, the American approach to India has, as viewed from New Delhi, conspicuously lacked in consistency and, therefore, in trustworthiness. Most objectionable to Indians is the not unfounded impression that today their country no longer counts much in the United States, one way or the other (the "benign neglect" syndrome). It is another matter whether Americans have good reasons to feel piqued as well.

This mixture of basic (not unconditional, however,) trust in the Russians and disappointment with the United States, which has even tried to intimidate the country by a gunboat policy, explains well enough why the Indians are less concerned about a Soviet naval presence than about an American one. Soviet ships are not perceived as a potential threat to national security, but

9For a recent example see her interview to Soviet Television; *Pravda*, 8 December 1975.

rather as insurance for it. Moreover, there is no Soviet naval base or base-like installation on Indian soil.[10]

Compared with pro-Western littoral states, India's position is just reversed. As long as the U.S. fleet sails in these waters, a Soviet presence is regarded as a necessary counterweight. Indian and Iranian leaders agree in their demand that the fleets of both superpowers should withdraw, but Delhi and Teheran diametrically disagree as to which fleet is the larger, or, rather, the real danger while they are present.

Although the USSR does not subscribe to the Peace Zone proposal, it tries to make political use of it. It is so hazy in substance that it can be matched with Moscow's equally woolly "collective security plan," although the two should be mutually excluded. When Leonid Brezhnev visited India in November 1973, there was in the joint Soviet-Indian declaration a short passage about the Peace Zone, cautiously worded but, of course, positive. This was taken up by *Izvestia's* political commentator V. Kudryavtsev and linked with Soviet planning. The Peace Zone "could become an integral part of the idea of an Asian collective security system which the Soviet Union has advanced and which is supported by many governmental and public circles in the Asian countries."[11]

Two concrete Soviet aims could be achieved by the littoral states' Peace Zone campaign in the UN and elsewhere. First, a growing condemnation of foreign powers' bases and important military installations. Since the U.S. has not concealed the nature of its facilities in the area (there has been so much first-hand official and competent unofficial comment that the world is well informed) it is relatively easy for the Soviets to draw Third World attention to these facts and to fall in step with the generally negative reactions. The Soviet Union will most probably never go on record admitting that its own facilities in Somalia and elsewhere have similar functions, so its advantage will remain: the United States has bases and the USSR takes a firm stand against them.

The second reason for Soviet siding with Peace Zone propagators is that denuclearization of the Indian Ocean has become an important part of the proposal. The USSR is bound to feel concerned about the strike capacity of Polaris/Poseidon submarines from the Indian Ocean against targets

---

[10]Vishakapatnam on the Gulf of Bengal which is often cited in Western publications as a Soviet facility cannot be seriously regarded as such; it might one day be made available for use by Soviet submarines, but this would require a shift in the policy of the Indian government.

[11]"The Indian Ocean in the Plans of Imperialism," *International Affairs*, November 1974, p. 118.

in the Soviet heartland.¹² Since the chances of Soviet ASW in such a large
area are slim, the USSR is interested in any form of international disapproval of a nuclear presence in the Indian Ocean. Consequently, the demand
for a denuclearized Indian Ocean has been part of the rhetoric in Sovietinspired international conferences in recent years.

For India, however, this concept has lost some flavor since a number
of Indian Ocean states, following Sri Lanka's initiative, have tried to extend
the Peace Zone to the littoral states themselves as far as nuclear weapons
are concerned, suggesting that all these countries should pledge to abstain
from their development or use. Pakistan made use of this move by formally
proposing in the United Nations' 29th session to declare South Asia a nuclearweapon free zone, analogous to similar proposed areas (Middle East, Africa,
Latin America). It was difficult for India to stave off such an obvious encroachment upon its nuclear option. The USSR and her allies supported
New Delhi.

To sum up, the USSR and India have important common interests regarding Indian Ocean policy: mainly to prevent a further consolidation
of U.S. positions, either by direct moves (e.g. Diego Garcia) or indirectly
via pro-Western states in the area. Both the USSR and India are aware that
the focus of U.S. regional interests has substantially shifted in recent years
to the Persian Gulf and that in this course new informal alignments have
become effective which are not favorable to their respective general policy
aims. The military build-up of the pro-Western or, to be precise, the clearly
not pro-Soviet Gulf states with their growing cooperation, must be regarded
by the Soviets with concern. To the Indians, Pakistan's involvement in this
process, from which it draws strength and the capacity to keep a distance
from the Indian field of gravity, is also a source of concern. Additionally
both the USSR and India have adopted policies to forestall and counteract
Chinese gains in Indian Ocean littoral states, as demonstrated by their concerted reaction to the events in Bangladesh after August 1975.

But there are also distinct divergences. To the USSR, the Indian Ocean
has become another area of rivalry with the United States. Therefore, the
presumed primary Soviet aim is to deny the Americans advantageous strategic positions which could be used directly against Soviet security interests.
This can be achieved by improving its own strategic and political posture, in
part by exploiting local or regional conflict situations.

¹²This subject has been discussed frequently in recent years; for an early assessment see: G. Jukes, "The Indian Ocean in Soviet Naval Policy," IISS *Adelphi Paper*
no. 87, May 1972.

India, for its part, denounces the use of the Indian Ocean for acts of superpower antagonism. At the same time, India hopes to build up its own maritime forces so that the claim of littoral states to be able to police the area alone, could gain conviction. In such a future development, India hopes to achieve a position of relative strength among the littoral states, a position to which the country feels entitled according to the consensus of its political elites.[13]

IDEOLOGICAL ASPECTS

Collective security for Asia (just as for Europe or elsewhere) is being regarded in Moscow as part of the historical process that is bound to favor the aims of the socialist camp in the global antagonism of class struggle. Détente is expected to sharpen this struggle. The Soviet Union has emerged, through acknowledged strategic parity with the United States, as the main supporting force for national liberation, or otherwise "just" wars. But wars, as opposed to other methods of sociopolitical change impart risks for the USSR.

According to the Soviet concept, the desired transformation of societies and governments in the Third World is to be achieved gradually, in step with the growth of the political consciousness of the masses. Along this way, the USSR supports "national-democratic, anti-imperialist" governments and, through its economic aid, strengthens the public industrial sector where proletarian consciousness is expected to develop rapidly. The accompanying advances of social and political mass organizations (trade unions, youth groups, USSR friendship societies, etc.) lead to the formation of a broad anti-imperialist front. Existing Communist or "revolutionary-democratic" parties act as an avantgarde and prepare the final stage before the overthrow of the right, reactionary classes; the final stage being the merger of all progressive parties and groups under the banner of scientific socialism. Actively supported by all socialist countries, this front would then be able to break reactionary resistance and take over the government, not necessarily in the name of Communism but drawing from this source its main inspiration and guidance.

Concerning Asia, an Indian expert on Soviet and Communist affairs offers this interpretation for the USSR's motivations. "Unlike the imperial-

[13]As an example, see the various contributions to an Indian Ocean seminar in New Delhi, edited by T.T. Poulose, *Indian Ocean Power Rivalry*, 1974, New Delhi. See also the various writings of K. Subrahmanyam, the former Director of the Institute for Defense Studies and Analysis, New Delhi.

ists, the Soviet Union comes to Asia not in search of markets and raw materials, nor to dominate peoples and societies, but to strengthen regimes that are willing to fight imperialism and neocolonialism and build independent national economies, and forces that are struggling to win social justice and equity for the masses."[14] It is worthwhile to compare these lofty Soviet aims with the realities on the Indian subcontinent. How far have they been vindicated? The balance sheet is, on the whole, negative. In recent times there have been substantial setbacks due to the elimination of pro-Moscow governments and political forces from various national scenes.

The case of Bangladesh has been mentioned above. The new leaders in Dacca no longer even pay lip-service to a Soviet brand of socialism. All former vestiges of a popular front of "progressive" parties and groupings (youth organizations, trade unions, etc.) with a tilt towards Moscow have vanished. To boost the weak economy, private investment is being strongly encouraged. Four years after the birth of Bangladesh midwifed by Moscow, the leftists who are left either look to Peking or cultivate an indigenous radical dogma.

Developments in Pakistan are also out of step with Moscow's views. The National Awami Party (NAP), with its strong links to Afghanistan and traditional sympathies for both the USSR and India, has been banned; its leaders under arrest or removed from the political scene. Cabinet ministers and other office-holders with ideas of social change reminiscent of Moscow-style communism are no longer in positions of political influence.

There is a similar development in Sri Lanka, where the Trotskyite ministers (basically pro-Soviet in spite of the Party's origin) have recently been removed from the coalition government. In that country, the Trotskyists have always regarded themselves more as the true guardians of dogmatic Marxist policies than the weaker pro-Moscow Communists. As a result of their clash with the government, Sri Lanka's Left has lost much of its power base.[15]

In Afghanistan, so close under Soviet surveillance, the so-called Central Committee of younger Officers that had come up with the "putsch" in July 1973 and was generally believed to have had strong Moscow leanings, has been outmaneuvered by President Daud during 1975. A cabinet reshuffle in

[14]Bhabani Sen Gupta, "The Insecurity of Asia: The View from Moscow," *Pacific Community*, January 1975, p. 260.

[15]M. Woollacott, "Bandaranaike coalition breaks up," *Guardian*, 30 August 1975.

late 1975 has led to a further removal of pro-Moscow elements.

All is not in favor for Moscow in India either. Although the struggle between Mrs. Gandhi and diverse forces opposing her has been decided overwhelmingly in her favor, much to the comfort of the USSR, this does not mean that the path has been cleared for the implementation of social change and radical reforms according to Soviet wishes as represented by the Communist Party of India (CPI).[16]

The Indian Prime Minister has emerged from this grave crisis with near dictatorial powers and in full command of the Congress Party. Thus the long-cherished hope of the Communists to move ever closer to the "progressive" wing of the Congress Party, thereby paving the way for some sort of a popular front and eliminating the "reactionary" forces from this all-embracing organization, has once more receded into the background. Mrs. Gandhi's twenty point economic and social program is being applauded by both the USSR and the Indian Communists, but not without reservations. There are some implications of it that are diametrically opposed to their beliefs; above all, the strengthening of the private sector of the economy and the virtual interdiction of the trade unions' fight for better working conditions.

Apart from this, it is not at all clear that even the most overdue social reforms which, by necessity, would be at the cost of the upper and middle classes, both urban and rural, will be carried out with speed and vigor. Mrs. Gandhi knows well enough (like so many leaders in the Third World) that any serious disruption of the existing distribution of property and power, in short, a revolutionary social change (in ideological terms the end product of the Soviet concept) would sooner rather than later crush her own power basis: i.e., the various strata of dominating groups and classes in the country which work together to preserve the existing social structure wherein all of them have a vital stake.

There is some grim determination in the way every South Asian government acts against "left extremists" who are out to destroy "the system". The Naxalites in India are a conspicuous example. The Sri Lanka government learned the lesson in 1971. In Bangladesh a similar scene was played out in 1971 and thereafter, and again in November 1975 when hard-core Leftists were suppressed by nationalist, "centrist" army forces. Pakistan, by

[16]To be distinguished clearly from the Communist Party of India (Marxist)—CPI(M) or CPM—which tries to steer an independent course between Moscow and Peking.

comparison, has been least affected, but is certainly not outside the danger zone.[17]

To combat such potentially aggressive force, South Asian governments have set up substantial instruments: intelligence services, police, paramilitary forces, and the army.[18] The swift suppression of all forms of protest or agitation in India after June 1975 is proof of the effectiveness of this system in a country where, formerly, public expression of political mood seemed to be part of its "political culture."

The USSR usually draws a distinctive line between organized leftists, preferably well-channeled into some pro-Moscow party, and "ultra-leftists" who, as a rule, are denounced as acting on behalf of Maoism and, consequently, of China. But such distinctions are increasingly difficult to make in this part of Asia. There are many leftist revolutionary groups and organizations, mostly acting now under cover, which are neither clearly oriented towards Moscow nor towards Peking. Organized indigenous socialism, sometimes even blended with religious elements, has been developing, and has been attractive to the young generation; notably in Sri Lanka, Bangladesh, and India.

There is a clear correlation between such movements and the little promise life holds out today to young people in extremely poor societies who have had access to some education. Social equity according to Soviet prescriptions can never reach them in their lifetime. Maoism offers straighter solutions, but Chinese official policy towards their countries has puzzled and repelled them. They have learned that, ultimately, all outside powers, however progressive and egalitarian they sound, have their own national interests uppermost in mind. These powers support Asian governments, if it suits their interests, however corrupt, antisocial and incompetent these governments may be.

Thus, there is an increasingly distinct dividing line in South Asia; not between "progressives" and "reactionaries" as Moscow perceives them, but between the established forces in government and politics along with all those who have a stake in supporting them on the one hand, and disillusioned, frustrated, and for the most part young people who are becoming more and

[17]For an interesting comparison and discussion of the ideological bases and consequent actions of South Asian governments, see: S.D. Muni, "India's Political Preferences in South Asia," *India Quarterly*, January–March 1975, pp. 23-35.

[18]As this author was told some years ago by a knowledgeable Indian personality, the Indian police force is being kept free from Communists, both party members and sympathizers.

more cynical about Socialist slogans. They desire more social justice and better material chances here and now. This "radicalism" is what their governments are afraid of and what the Soviets do not want to support. Things could get out of control and the substantial assets which the USSR has gathered in South Asia by cooperating with ruling groups and established parties could become endangered.

CONCLUSION

The USSR's interest in the area under discussion is to a great extent a function of geopolitical facts and strategic considerations. South Asia is adjacent to the tier that borders on the southern flank of the Soviet Union, from Turkey in the west to Pakistan in the east. Within the last decade, Moscow has tried, with considerable success, to neutralize the respective countries, so that they are no longer openly hostile to, and see the advantages of normal relations with the USSR; mainly through economic cooperation. The idea, ascribed to Mr. Kosygin in early 1969, to create some active economic partnership with the help of multilateral trade and traffic extending to the Indian subcontinent, has not materialized. However, the Soviet Union has not given it up; with changed conditions it might reemerge.

OPEC price policy after October 1973 has brought about some forces to countervail Soviet influence in this area. This comes from mainly Iran with its new consciousness as a regional power, but also from Arab states which gained influence in South Asia by their willingness to mitigate the grave impact of the new oil prices on the budgets of importing countries.

On the Indian subcontinent, the Soviets have recently lost some leverage. The favorable situation that prevailed after the partition of Pakistan, when Mr. Brezhnev had hoped for a speedy spreading of the collective security plan, has given way to adverse developments. The change of political orientation in Bangladesh was another proof of the fact that India was not in a position to become the accepted leading power in its subregion. On a strong India, however, the USSR has hinged its hopes for a solid connection in Asia.

The most reliable link between the Soviet Union and India is the one that is least talked about in both countries; the strategic and military one. To the USSR, India is important with regard to both its main global adversaries; China and the United States. To India, both are potentially hostile powers as well; China by land—over the crest of the Himalayas and on account of its nuclear armament—the United States from the sea, by its dominance in the Indian Ocean which would be more clearly established with a base in India's vicinity on Diego Garcia. Against both of these perceived threats, the Soviet Union provides the countervailing power and remains, therefore, vitally important so long as India is not in a position to develop its own credible defense or—vis-à-vis the United States—to summon political support (see the Indian Ocean Peace Zone proposal).

India's motivations are, however, not convergent with those of the USSR. While the latter is vying to forge an alliance with India (on the basis of the treaty of 1971) which would be a durable instrument for its own policy of counteracting both China and the United States in Asia, India sees this relationship in the light of a temporary advantage: to bridge a difficult stretch of time and development while India is still relatively weak, both economically and militarily, and thus not in a position to achieve its longer-range objective of becoming the acknowledged, undisputed leading power in the subregion as well as an important political factor in an all-Asian context. A reduction in the influence of external powers in the Indian Ocean area, the USSR included, would be a precondition to this.

In addition, India could never hope to become a power in Asia on the shoulders of the Soviet Union. On the contrary, in order to gain credibility in the region, it would have to prove its independence from Moscow. This seems to be impossible while relations with China continue to be cool. Thus, there is a vicious circle: India is regarded by China as a Soviet stooge while it is impossible for India to gain independence from the Soviet Union in view of a potential threat from China against which the Soviet connection is the only available insurance. So, the future Chinese policy on India will be the most important factor in these developments.

In the relationship between the USSR and South Asia there have also been recent setbacks in the ideological sphere. By comparison with other Third World societies, the Middle East included, South Asia offers some favorable conditions for Soviet inroads. Communist or otherwise "progressive" parties exist, some with a long tradition such as the Communist Party of India. In the early 1970s, progress in this field seemed to further Soviet goals of seeing these forces united in popular front fashion, gaining weight domestically, and increasingly closing ranks with the Socialist camp.

Moves in this direction have been stalled in individual countries (in Bangladesh, in Sri Lanka, somewhat differently in Pakistan also). But even in the most important state, in India, no real progress has been achieved in spite of Mrs. Gandhi's display of strength in mid-1975 which was so much applauded by Moscow. The basic contradiction remains: "national-democratic" governments profess socialism but are not willing to carry it through to its logical conclusion, i.e. to a revolutionary social change because such a development would necessarily bring about the end of the prevailing basic power structure. In all South Asian states this is neither feudal nor bourgeois, nor socialist, but is a mixture of all this, with traditional patterns of distribution of power, tinged by religion, caste, bonds of kinship, and "oriental despotism."

Consequently, even a country like India which gives much verbal support to the rallying slogans of anti-imperialism, anti-fascism, socialist pattern of society etc., seemingly in accordance with Soviet directives, is not seriously willing to oblige Moscow by switching over to radical changes in its sociopolitical set-up, as this would mean the end of the prevailing distribution of interior power. The Soviet Union, in view of this dilemma, chooses to deal with the given forces, since they at least guarantee cooperation in the direction of some basic Soviet foreign policy objectives (cf. an anti-Chinese, anti-American, and pro-Soviet stance of the Indian government).

Taken together, there are many restraints for the Soviets in this part of Asia, some of them, most probably, insurmountable. Their best assets are India's security perceptions and regional ambitions. But even India is not "safe" in the sense of an assured, close partnership for a long period to come. Thus, Moscow's high hopes and intentions of 1972, after the partition of Pakistan, have not materialized, mainly because developments within the region were much more complicated than could have been anticipated in Moscow. The plan for an Asian security system with a leading role for the USSR has become stuck, but remains on the Soviet agenda as a useful multipurpose tool.

On the other hand, the Soviet Union's stance in the area is by no means weak, if looked upon not in absolute but in relative terms. She is a power in Asia by virtue of her firm position in Soviet Central Asia and the various advantages derived from this; acquaintance with Asian mentality, geographical proximity, and the demonstration effect of a successful struggle against many plagues that still haunt the southern Asians.

Compared to China, the Soviet Union has a far greater potential for aid, trade, diplomatic leverage, and military power. This is being respected although it does not win friends. Compared to the United States, the Soviet approach to the area has been much more consistent, as it was less subject to global or domestic considerations alien to the area itself.

The Soviet Union at an early time chose India as the most important state in the region, and relations with the smaller countries were adjusted accordingly. This policy has basically paid off. India has remained, if not a friend, a trusting and trusted partner. The bizarre extremities of both China's and the West's changing attitudes towards India—from friendship and admiration to indifference, slight, and hostility—throw into relief Soviet behavior which, by any standards, seems to be more mature, displaying patience and understanding even in trying situations. Such psychological features should not be underrated by the advocates of Realpolitik.

Again, the Sino-Soviet conflict hampers the Russian's capability to keep their heads steadily above the clouds. They cannot but judge many developments by the unrealistic rules of this rivalry, in terms of a zero-sum game. Since there is not much prospect of a lessening of tensions between the two Communist giants, least of all in an area of equal geographical proximity to both of them, the Asian states are in the process of shaping their own philosophies with regard to the advantages and risks deriving from this Second Cold War.

Some Aspects
of Recent Soviet Policy
toward East and
Southeast Asia

Joachim Glaubitz

Two events that occurred in the first half of the 1970s have had a strong impact on the political and strategic situation of East and Southeast Asia. The surprisingly fast détente between China and the United States and the unexpectedly rapid end of the war in Indochina. The latter was followed by a complete withdrawal of American forces from continental Southeast Asia. The development that resulted from ·these events has fostered the Sino-Soviet rivalry in the Asia-Pacific region. The new chapter in the relations between China and the United States that was opened up in July 1971 by the secret visit of Henry Kissinger to the People's Republic of China provoked the Kremlin's fear of a Sino-American alliance against Soviet interests in Asia. The normalization of Sino-Japanese relations that followed only seven months after President Nixon's visit to China further nurtured Soviet suspicion and involved Japan in the rivalry between its two Communist neighbors. The following contribution analyzes how the Kremlin perceived the rapid change in the relationship between China on one side and the

United States and Japan on the other. It will further assess how Soviet policy tries to adopt to the new situation in Southeast Asia.

SOVIET PERCEPTION OF SINO-AMERICAN DETENTE

Years ago the Soviet Union realized the temporary nature of Sino-American antagonism. At the end of the Cultural Revolution in 1969, when the dispute with the Peking leaders seized upon issues of Chinese foreign policy, the Soviet Union made simultaneous remarks on the relationship between China and the United States. Its characterization might have been applied equally to its own relationship with the United States: shrill anti-Americanism in terms of propaganda, and coexistence in the sphere of concrete relations.[1]

A comprehensive analysis of the Sino-American relationship published in Moscow before Henry Kissinger made his secret visit to Peking in July 1971, lists six areas of potential, or actual, Sino-American understanding: the Taiwan issue, the Indo-Pakistan conflict, Vietnam, the question of United Action in Vietnam, Anti-Sovietism, and nuclear armament.[2]

Within the scope of this study, the last three items are of particular interest. They demonstrate, in an early stage, a motive in Soviet analysis of Sino-American relations that has been constantly repeated up to the present. In justifying its own rejection of United Action with the Soviet Union, China argued that the Soviet Union collaborated with the United States and wanted, by "United Action," to obliterate the line of demarcation between Marxist-Leninists and revisionists.[3]

The Chinese decision was in fact based on two considerations clearly appreciated by the Soviets:

1. Taking part in United Action might have resulted in getting China involved in an armed conflict with the United States. China wanted to avoid that risk.

2. United Action might have accelerated a solution to the Vietnam problem. Involvement in Vietnam, however, meant weakening the United States and discrediting its politics; morever, it promoted U.S. isolation in

[1]cf. *Kitaj segodnja* [*China Today*], Moscow, 1969, p. 243.

[2]*Vnesnaja politika KNR* [*China's Foreign Policy*], Moscow 1971, pp. 157-165.

[3]cf. "Refutation of the New Leaders of the CPSU on 'United Action' ", *Peking Review*, No. 46, 12 Nov. 1965, p. 12.

the field of foreign policy and finally made it more susceptible to China's demands.

Even at that time, Soviet analyses stated with some concern that China actually did not oppose the aggressive undertakings of the United States, but fought against the Soviet Union and the other Socialist countries.[4] Ever since the end of the 1960s, the growing hostility of Chinese policy vis-à-vis the Kremlin was labelled "Anti-Sovietism" and it was feared that the United States might profit by this contest. In the Soviet Union, it was understood that the United States would interpret the Sino-Soviet conflict as a manifestation of Chinese nationalism and might consequently expect a new balance of forces in the world, favorable to the United States. In this case, the Soviet Union would find itself in a disadvantageous strategic position. Thus, the Soviet Union concluded that the United States would have a long-term interest in consolidating the rift between China and the Soviet Union, and in preventing their returning to friendly terms.

The Kremlin was well aware that in order to disentangle Chinese foreign policy from its precarious double confrontation with the Soviet Union and the United States, Peking had attempted to increase the flexibility of its foreign policy by exacerbating its anti-Soviet strategy.[5]

The Soviet analysts have good reason not to make mention of the fact that it was the Soviet Union that gave the probably decisive impulse for an accelerated rapprochement between China and the United States. The Soviet-lead intervention of Warsaw Pact troops in the CSSR in August 1968 and its subsequent justification by the so-called Brezhnev Doctrine marked a turning-point of China's relations with the Soviet Union. Since the Kremlin reproached China with having betrayed the revolution and deviated from Marxism-Leninism, the Peking leaders had to consider their country a potential target for the Brezhnev Doctrine. The change in the Chinese perception of being menaced found expression in a new terminology: henceforth, in Chinese polemics the Soviet system was labeled as "Social Imperialism" and its leaders as "Social Imperialists". Vis-à-vis the United States, however, China indicated in as early as November 1968[6] that it would be prepared to discuss an agreement using as a basis the Five Principles of Peaceful Coexistence at the next ambassadorial-level meeting (in Warsaw, scheduled for February 1969).

[4]cf.*Vnesnaja politika KNR*, (henceforth: VP KNR), p. 163.
[5]cf. *VP KNR*, p. 164.
[6]cf.*Hsinhua News Agency*, Daily Bulletin No. 3952, 26-11-1968.

Even the mention of "peaceful coexistence" was remarkable during the final stage of the Cultural Revolution. The Soviet observers also perceived this noteworthy signal given by China, although they interpreted it as a reply to an offer made by President Nixon for direct contacts with China.[7] The explanation is not very convincing, considering that there had been direct American-Chinese contacts at ambassadorial level ever since 1955, and the Soviets themselves used to regard these talks as extraordinary, declaring: "No Socialist country, nor any of the countries that China regards as its allies in the struggle against American imperialism, enjoys such attention on the part of the Chinese government, or maintains with it diplomatic contacts of such intensity and on such a high level."[8]

The last of the areas of Sino-American understanding concerns nuclear armament. The Soviet Union has so far discussed in public questions related to Chinese nuclear armament with great restraint. The most detailed comments date back to the time before the détente initiated in connection with Henry Kissinger's secret visit to China. However, the various articles exemplify a shift of accent in the Soviet argumentation. It is quite revealing in this context to compare the statements of one and the same author over the period from 1969 to 1975. All his expositions reflect the basic view of an aggressive, chauvinistic, and consequently dangerous China.[9]

Initially the Soviet Union maintained that China's quest for a nuclear equilibrium with the United States would create a new foundation for the bilateral relations. The nuclear superiority of the United States was regarded as a catalyst of a Sino-American rapprochement in which both would be looking for opportunities of understanding.[10] Once such an understanding has been achieved, however, the Soviet Union warned the United States explicitly of the Chinese nuclear potential. China's nuclear armament, it argued, contained a calculated element of deterring an American nuclear attack, yet it remained a potential menace to the interests of the United States and their allies.[11]

---

[7]cf. S. Sergejcuk, SSaA i Kitaj [*U.S. and China*], 2nd ed., Moscow 1973, p. 188.

[8]Kitaj segodnja, *op.cit.*, p. 242-243 and—in a slightly modified version—*VP KNR*, p. 168.

[9]cf. *Ibid.*, p. 230; *VP KNR*, p. 149-150; Zanegin, B.N., "O nekotorych aspektach amerikano-kitajskich otnosenij," ("On some aspects of the Sino-American relationship") SSaA (USA) No. 2, Feb. 1975, p. 38.

[10]*VP KNR*, p. 164-165.

[11]Zanegin, B.N., *op.cit.*

Soviet analyses of the Chinese nuclear armament have become more objective during the course of time. In 1969, Mao's practice of lessening the tactical significance of nuclear arms was given a "propagandistic" purpose intended to diminish the negative effect of the Chinese nuclear arms on world public opinion.[12] Three years later, the same author omitted the expression "propagandistic," spoke of "repeated demonstrations of success in the build-up of a nuclear arsenal," and even mentioned the unilateral commitment of the Chinese governments to the principle of no-first-use of nuclear weapons.[13] The part the Soviet Union plays with regard to a China in possession of an increasing nuclear armament is seldom discussed. Only the Chinese rejection of the Soviet nuclear umbrella at the end of the 1950s is considered—in complete correspondence with western views—as evidence that China wanted to force the United States to acknowledge its stature and independence.[14]

The Soviet Union avoids speaking of a military threat emanating from China, or indicating a Soviet military threat against China. This may be demonstrated by the following examples: In 1969 a Russian study on China's nuclear armament and foreign policy stated: "China does not intend to give an occasion to the United States or other presumable adversaries to make use of their nuclear armament."[15] When the author repeated his statement three years later, he significantly omits the phrase "or other presumable adversaries."[16] The reason for this is clear. There is only one "presumable adversary" apart from the United States who might employ his nuclear weapons against China: the Soviet Union. The suggestion of a potential use of Soviet nuclear arms against China was deleted from the text because the Soviet Union probably wanted to avoid any cause of being reproached of applying nuclear threat.

The second example occurred at about the same time: When Erich Honecker, First Secretary of the East German SED, in May 1971 gave a speech to the Plenum of the Party Central Committee criticizing Peking and referring to the "strength of the community of the Socialist countries as a reliable wall" against China, the Soviet party newspaper skipped the reference to the "strength" because, as might be assumed, Moscow does not want

[12]Kitaj segodnja, *op.cit.*, p. 230.
[13]*VP KNR*, p. 164.
[14]*VP KNR*, p. 149.
[15]Kitaj segodnja, *op.cit.*, p. 230.
[16]*VP KNR*, p. 164.

any of its allies to lay stress on the military aspect, i.e., the role of the Warsaw Pact, in connection with China.[17]

The published Soviet analyses represent China without exception as a danger to other countries but not to the Soviet Union. This tendency has increased. As we have seen, even the United States is being warned at present that their interests are being menaced.

SOVIET WARNINGS TO THE UNITED STATES

In Soviet analyses, the President's trip to China receives heavy principal criticism. But whether the policy of the United States or the policy of the "Mao Tse-tung clique" are under review, each is reproached for having given up principles and made compromises. Only a few observers give a more objective argumentation. They hold the view that "at the preparatory stage of the Sino-American rapprochement (1969-1971), the initiative rested with the United States, whereas after the U.S. President's visit to Peking, the situation began to change."[18] This apparently is a tactical argument; for Moscow has realized what conclusions the Chinese leadership had drawn from the invasion into the CSSR and from its justification. Moreover, ten months later, in June 1969, the Soviet Union emphasized the growing interest it had in exerting its influence in the Asia-Pacific region by reviving its project for a system of collective security in Asia. Yet, at the same time, the United States, on its part, by proclaiming the Nixon Doctrine announced its gradual disengagement in Asia.

Consequently, Moscow's argument that the initiative for the Sino-American rapprochement had shifted from the United States to China ever since 1972 misrepresents the motives for this development. On the part of the Chinese, the détente in the Sino-American relations was the result of a reassessment of the Soviet threat, regardless of whether or not such a threat really existed. For the Americans, the rapprochement was the precondition for a way out of Vietnam. The coincidence of these very different motives finally led to a détente in the Sino-American confrontation.

The Soviet interpretation of this process reveals an apprehension that the Chinese diplomacy might be adroit to the American. B.N.

[17]cf. *Neues Deutschland*, May 4, 1971; *Pravda*, May 5, 1971, p. 4 Joachim Glaubitz: "The other German State and Asia," *Pacific Community*, Tokyo, vol. 3, No. 4, July 1972, p. 773.

[18]Zanegin, B.N., *Far Eastern Affairs*, Moscow, 1975/1, p. 74.

Zanegin, an expert on China in the Institute of the U.S.A., repeatedly criticizes the maneability of the United States policy and indicates possible repercussions on the Soviet-American relationship. "The Chinese moves to influence U.S. foreign policy and the connivance displayed by the United States Administration may threaten normalization with the USSR. Still, the U.S. Administration has shown a readiness to meet the PRC more than halfway and has done nothing about Peking and pro-Peking progaganda in the U.S.A., which affects Soviet interests."[19] Furthermore the U.S. government, in conformity with the negative Chinese approach, "has refrained from formulating its attitude towards the Soviet proposal for collective security in Asia."[20]

In suggesting the possibility of repercussions on the Soviet-American relationship, Zanegin attempts to restrict as far as possible the scope for further reconciliation between China and the United States. In this context, he announces "grave consequences" for international affairs, pointing out three areas—all of them focuses of American foreign policy—in which difficulties might arise:

1. The further normalization of the Soviet-U.S. relations might be impeded or interrupted which might result in a destabilization of the international situation;

2. in Southeast Asia, the formation of an opposition directed against the United States might occur, and American influence be reduced; the increasing doubts in U.S. commitments and the fear of an economic expansion by Japan might subsequently favor a situation in which China would get control over the region;

3. an intensification of the U.S.-Japanese contradictions could not be excluded whereas the contradictions with China would be maintained and become more effective as soon as the United States' position would lend itself to possible attack.

This catalogue of potential difficulties reflects the Soviet apprehension that China's influence in Asia might rapidly increase, since by the détente or normalization of its relations with the U.S. and Japan their earlier resistance would be reduced. Soviet apprehension at the Sino-American reconciliation is of such intensity that a serious disturbance of the bilateral détente between the Soviet Union and the United States cannot be ruled out.

[19]*Ibid.*, p. 75.
[20]*Ibid*, p. 76.

On the other hand, the Soviet Union assumes that the American political assistance for China will not go beyond the point where the interest of the U.S. in maintaining the balance of power is affected, i.e., where the process of U.S.-Soviet détente is at stake. The Soviet side has realized that in this way it is in a position of introducing an "element of uncertainty" into the Sino-American relations which enables it to impart a degree of influence on these relations.

Actually the Soviet Union seems to be afraid lest American technology would not promote a rapid development of the Chinese industrial and armament potential. This can be seen in Soviet reviews of the Sino-American economic relations which exclusively mention goods of a certain strategic importance, as e.g., the supply of Boeing 707 airliners, Lockheed transports, or the Chinese negotiations with American firms regarding drilling equipment for the exploitation of off-shore oil.

SOVIET RESPONSE TO CHINA'S DRIVE SOUTHWARD

Because of the secret nature of numerous Sino-American talks, the USSR is afraid of the region being ultimately divided into spheres of influence that are bound to run against Soviet interests.[21] The most recent Soviet analysis concerning the issue of Sino-American collusion goes still further. When in January 1974 Chinese naval units in the struggle against South Vietnamese armed forces conquered the Paracel Islands in the South China Sea, about 350 km south of Hainan, Washington kept silent. For its part, Peking refrained from criticism when the United States, in agreement with Great Britain, decided to construct a base on Diego Garcia in the Indian Ocean. The American silence on the occasion of the Chinese occupying, and confirming their claim to, the Paracel Islands was sufficient reason for the Soviet Union to maintain that a "Sino-American condominium" was emerging.[22]

China's claim for almost the whole of the South China Sea with its islands and reefs is of extraordinary strategic significance. If China succeeds in enforcing this claim against neighboring states, especially Vietnam, it will take control of the most important sea routes between the Pacific and Indian Oceans. Even today, with the Paracel Islands being in firm Chinese control, it possesses an important observation post in the South China Sea. Besides

[21]cf. Sergejcuk, *op.cit.*, p. 217.
[22]Zanegin, B.N., *op.cit.*, SSaA No. 2, Feb. 1975, p. 40.

its strategic value the South China Sea may be of particular interest to China because of reportedly rich oil deposits.

The Soviet Union has realized that the Chinese presence in the South China Sea might result in restricting the manoeuverability of its Pacific fleet. It seems to regard the build-up of the Chinese navy to be as great a threat to its interests as the situation at the boundaries; the expansion of the Chinese naval force "reflects the general direction of the build-up of the armed forces of the People's Republic of China."[23] This assessment of the Chinese interests, and the silence on the part of the U.S. government regarding Peking's claims, foster Soviet suspicions of a far-reaching coincidence of Chinese and U.S. strategic interests in this region. China's tenacity in advocating its claims in the South China Sea, as well as the consequences it might have for the Soviet interests in Asia, caused the Kremlin to dissociate itself from the position it had originally held in the question of the Chinese claims.

On 5 September 1951, during the negotiations on a peace treaty with Japan, Andrei Gromyko, head of the Soviet delegation in San Francisco, stated the attitude of his government. He explicitly pleaded for China's right to its territories that had so far been detached from it: "It is an uncontested fact that China's very own territories it has been deprived of, as the Isle of Formosa, the Pescadores, the Paracel Islands, and other territories, have to be returned to the Chinese [People's] Republic."[24] The Soviet amendments for the peace treaty with Japan demanded the acknowledgment of the full sovereignty of the People's Republic of China among others over the Pratas and Paracel Islands, the Macclesfield Bank, and the Spratley Islands.[25] As late as 1959, a Soviet handbook on China still contained a map on which both the Paracel and the Spratley Islands, which are situated in the Southern part of the South China Sea, are marked as being Chinese.[26] This corresponds precisely with the claims China has put forward up to the present.

When in January 1974 China conquered the Paracel Islands, which were claimed by Vietnam as well, the Soviet Union condemned the Chinese move but did not comment on the issue of the title to the territory.[27] These tactics of the Kremlin can be traced until recently. At the end of November 1975, a Soviet polemic dealing with "Peking's hegemonistic efforts" con-

[23] *Ibid.*, p. 37.
[24] *Pravda*, 7 September 1951, p. 3.
[25] *Ibid.*, p. 4.
[26] cf. *Nas drug Kitaj* (Our Friend China), Moscow 1959, p. 1.
[27] cf. *Pravda*, 21 January 1974, p. 3.

tained a passage that the Vietnamese people regarded the Paracel Islands as its own territory.[28] Such a statement, it is true, cannot testify for the legitimacy of the Vietnamese point of view, but, considering the acute criticism of the Chinese action, the Soviet statement reads like a support for the Vietnamese claims. It is precisely this course which the Soviet leadership probably intends to produce. The remarkable modification of its stand on the issue of the islands is evidence that a Soviet policy regarding East and Southeast Asia is directed against China, the most influential counterpoint to the Soviet Union in the region.

CONCEPTS FOR MUTUAL CONTAINMENT: THE SOVIET MOVE

The Communist victory in Vietnam, and the withdrawal of the U.S. armed forces from Indochina, resulted in a marked intensification of the Sino-Soviet conflict in the Asia-Pacific region. Both sides have given an exposition of their conceptions of an Asia policy in the course of the last years: Ever since 1969, the Soviet Union has renewed its proposal of establishing a system of collective security in Asia. Since 1973, China has been soliciting a formula which specifically rejects hegemonistic efforts on the part of third countries in Asia and calls for united action against such efforts. Each side regards the other as its main adversary; containing its influence is the principal objective of their respective strategies.

Ever since Brezhnev spoke of creating a system of collective security for Asia in 1969, the Soviet Union has propagated this idea with growing intensity; now it has become a central element of the Soviet Asia policy.[29] In the course of time, the original proposal has been developed and complemented; particularly in August 1973 when Brezhnev spoke in Alma-Ata.[30] The result is a catalogue of principles that are also part of the Principles of Peaceful Coexistence. However, there is no definition or conceptualization of a "system" or of "collective security." "Collective security" is realized, conventionally within a collective defense alliance. The Soviet Union, however, has not yet discussed the military aspects of its proposal. It demands,

---

[28]*Ibid.*, 22 November 1975, p. 5. A TASS report of 27 Nov. 1975 claimed that the Spratley Islands "do not belong to China" cf. *China News Summary* No. 598, January 14, 1976, p. 3.

[29]cf. Dieter Braun and Joachim Glaubitz, *Europa Archiv*, Folge 1, 1974, p. 22-32.

[30]cf. *Pravda*, 16 August 1975, p. 2.

indeed, the abolition of foreign military bases and the dissolution of the military-political alliances in Asia as preconditions for collective security in Asia, but it is vague about what is intended instead to provide physical security.[31]

A tactical aspect of the Soviet proposal lies in the attempt to present certain patterns in order to legitimate the idea of collective security. For years the Soviet Union has been endeavoring to attach greater importance to its proposal by referring to the 1930s when the idea of collective security originated, and by presenting itself as the creator and indefatigable promoter of this idea.[32] Reference to two model conferences assist in vesting this issue of the Soviet-Asia policy with historical continuity, i.e.: The Bandung Conference of 1955, and the CSCE in Helsinki. This tactical measure is intended to promote the following three objectives:

In the first place, the Asian countries are to be reminded of the fact that they have already formulated such principles as have met with the approval of the Soviet Union and consequently are also consistent with the idea of collective security. Thus the Soviets want to make their proposal for a system of collective security more easily acceptable.

Secondly, the reference to the Afro-Asian Conference in Bandung has the purpose of gradually preparing the public for accepting also African countries under the Soviet proposal. In this context, an article of Soviet origin pointed out that "the establishment of a system for collective security in Asia fully corresponds to the initiative of a number of Afro-Asian countries (India, Ceylon, Tanzania, and others)."[33]

Thirdly, the inclusion of Bandung and Helsinki in the Soviet proposal and the amalgamation of the conference results as it has recently been effected[34] is to convince the Asian countries that agreements which were worked out for Europe can be conveyed to Asia as well. This intention can be verified at present in Soviet comments relating to collective security in Asia. Ever since the conclusion of the Helsinki conference, it is regularly

---

[31]cf. Vorontsov, V.B. and D.T. Kapustin, "Kollektivnaja bezopasnost' v Azii. Istorija i sovremennost'" (Collective Security in Asia. History and Present Time). *Problemy Dal'nego Vostoka*, No. 4, 1975, p. 49.

[32]cf. *Pravda*, 21 August 1973, p. 4, and recently Vorontsov and Kapustin, *op.cit.*, p. 40.

[33]Mikhailova, M., "The Bandung Principles and China's Great-Power Course in the 'Third World'". *Far Eastern Affairs*, No. 3, 1975, p. 34.

[34]cf. Vorontsov and Kapustin, *op.cit.*, pp. 44-47.

pointed out that the ten principles of the Final Act of the CSCE are not only applicable to Europe but also to other continents.[35]

Last, but not least, the Soviet Union firmly stresses the inviolability of frontiers incorporated into the catalogue of principles at the conferences of Bandung as well as of Helsinki. Since the Kremlin is involved in territorial disputes with Japan and China it is keenly interested in this principle. This crucial issue will be dealt with later in the book.

The Soviet tactics of relying on Bandung and Helsinki has its weak points. As an allegedly non-Asian country, the Soviet Union could not take part in the Bandung Conference. This precedent can be used against its presently intensified efforts to become accepted as an Asian country itself. The Soviet Union's subsequent attempts of disparaging the role of China on the Bandung conference reveal the anti-China tendency of its Asia policy.[36] With most of the Asian countries, this procedure has had a rather counterproductive effect.

After all, the final communiqué of the Bandung conference contains a paragraph that can quite easily be employed against the core of the Soviet Asia policy. It relates to the "renunciation of agreements on collective defense which serve the particular interests of any of the great powers."[37] It is symptomatic that this point is not being mentioned in the Soviet attempt of bringing the principles of Bandung and Helsinki into accordance with each other.[38]

An important result of the Helsinki conference for the Soviet side was the incorporation of a guarantee of the Western frontiers of its sphere of influence and control. In the Soviet proposal for the security of Asia, the territorial inviolability equally plays an essential part. Asian countries with unsettled territorial issues between themselves and the Soviet Union should be aware that the Kremlin will strive for the territorial status quo in Asia by means of promoting collective security. In the case of Japan, for example, support for the Soviet proposal would entail renouncing the four islands at the southern end of the Kuriles.

Concerning its Japan policy, the Soviet Union finds itself in a difficult situation. If it yields to the Japanese claims it would give up its principle

[35]cf. Kudryavtsev, V., *Izvestia*, 28 August 1975, p. 4.

[36]cf. Mikhailova, M., *op.cit.*, p. 27-29.

[37]Communiqué of the Afro-Asian Conference of Bandung, 24 April 1955, *Europa Archiv*, 20 May 1955, p. 7567.

[38]cf. Vorontsov and Kapustin, *op.cit.*, p. 45-46.

of the unviolability of post-war frontiers which it has so successfully defended in Europe. In that case, it would have to face corresponding claims in Europe which in Moscow would be considered a serious jeopardy to Soviet security interests. For example, *Pravda* commentator Viktor Majevskij remarked that the mere raising of the Kuriles issue was an effort to "revise the boundaries of Japan, an attempt that has something in common with the claims that the revanchists in Bonn enter in connection with Europe."[39]

Finally, yielding to Japan would prejudice the Soviet position in the current boundary negotiations with China. This attitude has not been modified up to the present. The Soviet Union is very anxious to avoid any reference to the still-unsolved territorial issue in Japanese-Soviet communiqués. In this context too, the Soviet Union tries to manipulate history.

In an agreement on the resumption of diplomatic relations with Japan from 19 October 1956, the Soviet Union stated its readiness to return to Japan the two islands at the southern end of the Kuriles after conclusion of a peace treaty.[40] But already in January 1960, after the revision of the Japanese-American security treaty, the Soviet government declared that the islands could not be returned until all U.S. forces would be withdrawn from Japan. At present, even this condition is not mentioned any more. In the most recent edition of the Diplomatic Dictionary which is edited by Gromyko, the reference to the possible reversion to Japan of Habomai and Shikotan as it was still printed in the 1964 edition, has been canceled.[41]

On the other hand, the Soviet inflexibility may cause a race between China and the Soviet Union for a peace treaty with Japan to be decided in favor of China, for every Japanese government has so far made the reversion of the four islands a precondition for the conclusion of a peace treaty with the Soviet Union. Moreover, Moscow cannot count upon Japanese support for a collective security system as long as the territorial issue remains unsolved.

Consequently, the peculiar nature of the situation in Asia is emphasized in Tokyo. They maintain that European solutions cannot simply be transferred to Asia. It should be remembered after all that Asia itself is not a homogeneous structure, but has to cope with a variety of problems according to the differences of their origins and characteristic features. To Japan, the dissolution of military blocs and bases as a precondition for the realiza-

[39]*Pravda*, 29 December 1967, p. 5.

[40]*Ibid.*, 20 October 1956.

[41]cf. *Diplomaticeskij Slovar'*, (Diplomatic Dictionary), Vol. 3, Moscow 1964 and 1973, p. 293 and p. 386 respectively.

tion of the Soviet plan is a further precarious issue. Its fulfillment would end the defense alliances between the United States, South Korea, and Japan and indeed leave the two countries without protection. These objections have a particularly unfavorable impact in Soviet goals, since they are voiced by the leading economic power in Asia whose support for a collective security system is especially important to Moscow.

A further precondition for the realization of the Soviet proposal pointed out by the Kremlin is the installation of a network of economic relations as well as the expansion and intensification of mutual economic cooperation. It must be mentioned that such cooperation is only applied to the developing countries and the countries within the Socialist system, whereas the role of the non-Socialist countries is being ignored or mentioned under critical commentaries in Soviet writings.[42]

According to Soviet perceptions, economic cooperation is to be intensified by means of the activation of existing regional organization. Two organizations in particular appear to be appropriate in Soviet eyes: The Regional Cooperation for Development (RCD), to which the Western Asian states Iran, Turkey, and Pakistan belong, and the Association of southeast Asian Nations (ASEAN) with Malaysia, Thailand, Singapore, Indonesia, and the Philippines as member states.

Regarding ASEAN, it is noteworthy that the extent to which the Soviet Union, in trying to expand and intensify its relations with the countries of Southeast Asia, is modifying its assessment of ASEAN. Originally, ASEAN, which was founded in 1967, in the Soviet view was an organization with economic and cultural objectives that were linked to secret plans for a political and military alliance with the United States.[43] As late as 1972, ASEAN is connected in Soviet studies with military alliance in Asia.[44] Yet in 1972 the Kremlin started a gradual revision of this position. This signal was given by the Soviet party organ with an altogether positive appreciation of the conference of the member states of ASEAN in Kuala Lumpur in December 1971.[45]

From now on, ASEAN reinterpreted a preparatory element for a collec-

---

[42]Vorontsov and Kapustin, *op.cit.*, p. 49.

[43]cf. *Diplomaticeskij Slovar'*, Moscow 1971, Vol. I, p. 158.

[44]cf. A.P. Markov "Voennye bloki v Azii i amerikano-kitajskie otnosenija" (Military Blocks in Asia and the Sino-American Relations), *Problemy Dal'nego Vostoka*, No. 1, 1972, p. 80.

[45]cf. *Pravda*, 27 December 1971, p. 3.

tive security system in Asia. The organization was to weaken the "position of imperialism" in the region of intensifying economic cooperation between the member states. For any further development, the Soviet Union recommended itself as a "natural and disinterested partner of the Asian countries.[46]

The Soviet Union pursues the long-term objective of eliminating "the one-sided character of their economic ties," i.e., the economic relations of the ASEAN states with non-Socialist countries like the United States and Japan, which are gradually to be substituted by economic links with the Soviet Union and the Socialist countries.[47] These are to be "completely new international economic relations"; just as in the political field the creation of a system of collective security "calls for the reorganization (preobrazovanie) of the total structure of the intra-State relations in Asia.[48] Even the most detailed Soviet presentations, however, leave it open to question what the actual structure of those relations shall be.

In addition to the vagueness of the Soviet proposal, a suspicion that the project might in reality be directed against China has caused the Asian countries to be rather cautious. They insist on China being included as a member of such a system. The Soviet Union on its part has asserted again and again that no state shall be excluded from membership, and it is taken for granted that China, too, is to take part in it. By these tactics, the Soviet Union tries to mark China as an enemy to any détente in Asia. On the other hand, it makes any positive progress in the discussion on its security system dependent on whether the leaders in Peking are prepared to take part in it.

Considering that China has rejected the proposal of a security system with utmost stringency since 1969 and still regards it as a project directed against itself, any support of the Soviet proposal would be interpreted in Peking as an anti-Chinese decision. In light of the objections mentioned above, this endorsement can be expected neither from Japan nor from other states neighboring China. Apart from the Mongolian People's Republic which is dependent upon the Soviet Union, no other country of Southeast or East Asia, including the Communist governments of Vietnam and Korea has so far stood out for the idea propagated by the Soviet Union.

[46]Vorontsov and Kapustin, *op.cit.*, p. 51.

[47]V. Pavlovskij, *Azii—Kollektivnuju Bezopasnost'* (Collective Security for Asia), Moscow 1974, p. 74.

[48]*Ibid.*, p. 71 and 79.

CONCEPTS OF MUTUAL
CONSTRAINT: THE CHINESE MOVE

In order not merely to reject the Soviet proposal, China developed a conception of its own concerning Asia. In this endeavor, it has proceeded with far more pragmatism than the Soviet Union. The Chinese do not attempt to offer their neighboring states any "system" for solving the regional problems. They offer the simple axiom of rejecting the campaign for hegemony on the part of third states or groups of states. At first glance, the Soviet Union's position appears to be the more positive compared with China, since it stands for something and China merely rejects a certain form of domination. But political reality has confirmed that it is easier for men to agree on what they reject than to determine what they want.

The renunciation of hegemony and the rejection of third countries' or groups of countries' dominance hegemony—the so-called hegemony clause— was first included in the Shanghai Communiqué of February 1972, signed by President Nixon and Premier Chou En-lai. Hegemony according to the Chinese definition means "expansion of power politically and economically, and exercise of control.[49]

According to Chinese literature, the hegemony clause was originally proposed by Henry Kissinger, and finally accepted after Mao Tse-tung had consented.[50] When Premier Tanaka, in September 1972, signed a Joint Statement on the normalization of Sino-Japanese relations the hegemony clause from the Shanghai Communiqué was included verbatim. This procedure revealed that this formula is of central significance to Chinese foreign policy.

It is surprising that Soviet analyses of Nixon's China trip initially ignored this point of the Shanghai Communiqué,[51] or at least merely took notice of the statement on hegemony which they considered untrustworthy.[52] Not until it became evident in the course of negotiations on a Peace and Friendship Treaty with Japan that China attached such immense importance on the inclusion of the hegemony clause was the political nature of the formula realized in Moscow as well. The conclusions drawn by Soviet observers were correct: an agreement with the United States on the renuncia-

---

[49]cf. *Tokyo Shimbun*, Evening Edition, April 26, 1975. Translated in Daily Summary of the Japanese Press, May 7, 1975, p. 5.

[50]*Asahi Shimbun*, Evening Edition, April 26, 1975, p. 2.

[51]cf. Sergejouk, *op.cit.*, p. 214-221.

[52]cf. J.D. Dmitriev, "Posle vizita premiera Tanaki v Pekin" (After Premier Tanaka's Visit to Peking), *Problemy Dal'nego Vostoka*, No. 1, 1973, p. 70-71.

tion of hegemony equated to U.S. recognition of China as a power equal to itself and support for China's attempt to enhance its status.[53] Incorporating the hegemony clause in the Japanese Peace and Friendship Treaty was regarded as an effort to bind Japan to an anti-Soviet policy.[54]

If China succeeded in persuading Japan to accept the hegemony clause in the Peace and Friendship Treaty, the anti-hegemony formulas would for the first time be incorporated in an international treaty. In the light of the uncompromising Soviet attitude in the Kuriles issue which was demonstrated again on the occasion of the Soviet Foreign Minister's visit to Japan, in January 1976, the conclusion of a Sino-Japanese treaty has drawn nearer to realization. Such a treaty will have the effect of bringing Japan closer to China, and it will at least for some time prejudice the Japanese-Soviet relations.

It seems at present as if the Kremlin based its Japan-policy on the assumption that yielding on the territorial question would not induce Japan to move further from China. China has the advantage of profiting from common cultural foundations and quiet complex on the part of Japan. This means that Japan and China are linked by a "special relationship" to which the Soviet Union has no alternative to offer. Even the Soviet attempts to make Japan a partner, on a large scale, in the development of Siberia are of limited value to Japan, since it cannot accept participation in projects of strategic importance without provoking China's protest.

Thus there is hardly any chance for preventing a solidification of relations between China and Japan. The only instruments presently used by the Kremlin with the aim of obstructing a closer Sino-Japanese understanding are diplomatic interventions connected with the explicit warning of a deterioration of Soviet-Japanese relations, and the increased demonstration of military presence in the North Pacific.

The Soviet Union is apprehensive of close cooperation between China, a country rich in labor and crude oil, and the highly industrialized Japan which is in urgent need of raw materials. Such an alliance would run counter to the Soviet Union's ambitions of intensifying its influence in the Asia-Pacific region. China on its part seems to pursue two objectives in its policy towards Japan:

53cf. B.N. Zanegin, "Sino-U.S. Rapprochement: What It is and Why," *Far Eastern Affairs*, No. 1, 1975, p. 79.

54cf. N.N. Nikolaev, B.V. Andreev, "Kitajsko-japonskie peregovory o zakljucenii dogovora o mire i druzbe" (Sino-Japanese Talks on the Conclusion of a Peace and Friendship Treaty), *Promlemy Dal'nego Vostoka*, No. 3, 1975, p. 67-72.

1. Using Japan's technological and industrial potential and persuading it at the same time to pursue a pro-China policy.

2. Preventing the development of too close economic and political relations between the Soviet Union and Japan.

This explains the intensity of China's support for the Japanese territorial claims vis-à-vis the Soviet Union: in this way, it stiffens the Soviet attitude and thus complicates the solution of the problem.

For Japan, too, it is rather advantageous—considering the present constellation of interests in the Asia-Pacific region—to leave the territorial issue unresolved but continue at the same time to demand its solution. By these tactics, Japan establishes an alibi for the amelioration of its relations with China. In other words maintaining this relaxed confrontation provides the Japanese policy with a greater scope of maneuverability towards the Kremlin.

Besides Japan, the whole ASEAN region as well as Indochina are areas of increasing Sino-Soviet rivalry. With striking similarity to Soviet tactics China, too, revised its view on ASEAN. When the organization was founded in 1967 the Chinese called it "an out-and-out counter-revolutionary alliance rigged up to oppose China, communism and the people." On this occasion the governments of the member states were considered "U.S. imperialism's running dogs in Southeast Asia."[55]

When the Kremlin changed its stand on ASEAN Peking followed suit. At the beginning of 1973 the Chinese press withholding any criticism, quoted the desire of ASEAN "to limit outside interference in the affairs of Southeast Asia," and "to make the area a zone of peace, freedom and neutrality."[56] Today these goals are openly defended by Peking against the Soviet moves to include the neutralization of Southeast Asia into its proposal for collective security.[57]

China has tried ever since 1972 to incorporate in communiqués and statements with heads of government some clause condemning hegemonistic endeavors of third countries. Although the anti-Soviet nature of this clause is quite apparent, the Chinese succeeded within two years, from 1973 to 1975, in incorporating the hegemony clause in 19 government or press communiqués, 12 of them signed with Asian countries. Compared with the

55*Peking Review* No. 34, 1967, p. 39-40.
56*Ibid.*, No. 6, 1973, p. 21.
57*Ibid.*, No. 33, 1975, p. 21.

abortive Soviet efforts of propagating their system of collective security in Asia, the diplomatic success of the Chinese is striking.[58]

It deserves notice that China between 1973 and 1975 signed communiqués with three ASEAN member states Malaysia, Thailand, and the Philippines in order to open diplomatic relations. In all these cases the signatories agreed on a strong anti-hegemony clause with identical wording, opposed both the striving for hegemony and establishing spheres of influence "in any part of the world," which points to the global aspect of China's policy against hegemony. The Sino-Philippine communiqué further states the readiness of both governments to cooperate in order to reach this goal.[59] Burma, Cambodia, Nepal, and Pakistan also agreed with China to oppose hegemony. If one accepts the view that there is political significance in those communiqués then the distribution of hegemony clauses reflects the degree of influence China exercises on the general foreign policy line of the countries in the Asia-Pacific region.

The self-confident Kim Il Sung of North Korea obviously did not agree to include a hegemony clause in the communiqué he signed in Peking in April 1975.[60] Vietnam's Le Duan, First Secretary of the Vietnamese Labor Party, could not agree with his Chinese hosts on any communiqué when he visited Peking in September 1975, especially on China's criticism of hegemony. A few weeks later in Moscow, however, he signed a lengthy "Soviet-Vietnamese Declaration" supporting the Soviet achievements in Helsinki. Although the declaration refers to the situation and future development in Southeast and East Asia, Le Duan did not commit himself to collective security in Asia.[61]

This might indicate that, at least for the time being, the Vietnamese leadership does not want to antagonize China. One cannot exclude the possibility however, that the uncompromising Chinese stand on the islands of the South China Sea may lead to a further deterioration of Sino-Vietnamese relations. In that case the Kremlin would probably try to obtain Hanoi's

[58]For details see Joachim Glaubitz, "Anti-Hegemony Formulas as Elements of Chinese Foreign Policy," *Asian Survey*, March 1976.

[59]*Peking Review*, No. 24, 1975, p. 8.

[60]*Ibid.*, No. 17, 1975, p. 12.

[61]*Pravda*, 31 October 1975, p. 1-2.

approval of the idea of Asian collective security in exchange for Soviet support to the Vietnamese territorial claim against China.

The Declaration signed by Brezhnev and Le Duan also included another point of possible disagreement with China's policy toward Indochina. The foreign policy orientation of future Laos and Cambodia as mentioned in the Declaration differ from Chinese notions on a decisive point. Chinese statements describing the future of both Indochinese countries always use the term "neutral," which was not incorporated in the Declaration.[62] China is firmly in favor of a large area of neutrality in Southeast Asia—the ASEAN region plus Laos and Cambodia—because neutral countries would serve as an obstacle to the spread of Soviet influence. Further, neutral countries close to China would hesitate to take up an unfriendly attitude towards a neighbor as powerful as China.

TOWARDS A TACIT U.S.-CHINESE ACCORD

President Ford's "Pacific Doctrine" announced in December 1975 has added another impediment to the difficulties which China is creating for Soviet policy in the Asia-Pacific region: the Soviets had to realize that the interests of the United States and China in East and Southeast Asia in some essential areas are in accord with each other. Both are interested in a continued military presence in the region, in maintaining the strength of the U.S.-Japanese alliance, and in pursuing a policy on the Korean peninsula that is acceptable to both governments in the North and in the South. Both Americans and Chinese consider an early withdrawal of U.S. forces from South Korea and the Philippines a risk to the existing balance of power (nor is the Soviet Union interested in jeopardizing this balance since it could lead to a confrontation with the United States).

The Pacific Doctrine, composed of six points, stresses in item 5 that a "peace in Asia depends upon a resolution of outstanding political conflicts." This principle is counter to the Soviet concept of collective security. For the solution of existing problems in Asia, the USSR proposes creation of its security system. The Americans, on the contrary, consider the solution of the existing problems a precondition for peace in Asia.

The sixth item of the Doctrine may be regarded as a counter-position to the Soviet ideas as well. "Peace in Asia requires a structure of economic

62*Pravda*, 31 October 1975, pp. 1-2.

cooperation reflecting the aspirations of all the peoples in the region."[63] It is not yet known what the structure of economic cooperation shall be, but taking notice of the Soviet plans of cooperation it may be assumed that the U.S. notion is opposed to those of the Soviet Union in this question.

Reactions from Peking and Moscow to the Pacific Doctrine were remarkable. China kept silent, and it is taken for granted that the leaders in Peking were informed beforehand of the American concept by President Ford and his Foreign Minister. This assumption is supported by a remark made by a member of the delegation accompanying President Ford, to the effect that the Chinese side had indicated that it would do nothing that might weaken the American position in the Philippines, Japan, Thailand, or anywhere else in Southeast Asia.

Moscow's reaction, on the other hand, was a distinct rejection of the Pacific Doctrine. The current commentaries especially criticize the apparent accord of Chinese and American interests and the resulting approval of U.S. military presence in Asia. To Soviet observers, the new doctrine is an attempt of exercising hegemony in the Pacific region and in Southeast Asia. This statement is an obvious allusion to the rejection of hegemony expressed by both Vice Premier Teng Hsiao-ping and President Ford.[64]

The positive reception of the Pacific Doctrine throughout Asia—even in the Japanese press which is generally critical of the United States—must have brought home again to the leaders in Moscow that their political and economic policies for East Asia and insular Southeast Asia still have considerable obstacles to overcome. Even in Vietnam and Laos, the last word on the extent of the Soviet influence has not yet been spoken.

[63]*International Herald Tribune,* 10 December 1975, p. 3; the other four points are: 1. American strength is basic to any stable balance of power in the Pacific; 2. Partnership with Japan is a pillar of U.S. strategy; 3. Normalization of relations with the People's Republic of China; 4. Stability and security of Southeast Asia as a continuing stake of U.S. policy.

[64]*Izvestia,* 16 December 1975, p. 3.

Soviet-American Bilateralism: Constraint on Soviet Behavior?

Uwe Nerlich

THE PROBLEM

Much of the Western public debate on Soviet power and détente is polarized around two views: (1) Détente policies currently offer no options or may even be inadvisable because of growing Soviet power and influence, (2) or else that for whatever reasons the Soviet Union is more likely than in the past to accommodate or to have vested interests in cooperative relations with the West (e.g., because Moscow now feels more secure as a result of its growing power). Whatever the shortcomings of and, indeed, domestic obstacles to Henry Kissinger's negotiating policies toward Moscow, his basic assessment seems to be more realistic than the characteristic "conservative" and "liberal" views. Soviet power and influence are expanding in ways that are anything but reassuring. But it is precisely for this reason that incentives have to be generated to integrate the Soviet Union to the extent possible into a system of agreed rules of behavior. The prospects may be modest, but the failure to achieve anything is likely to be worse. Western power is the backbone of any such effort, but exclusive reliance on strength and unilateralism may suffice in extreme cases, whereas Soviet power in more tangible situations would more or less go unchecked without constraint which could be induced by shaping the Soviet international environment.

Whether or not Soviet choices in a given situation will be shaped by what is expected to be a constraining factor will depend on tactical considerations as well as on perceived basic priorities of Soviet policies. The following is a general discussion of how Soviet risk-taking relates to issues of priorities, the types of contingencies expected from a Western point of view, what kinds of constraints and thresholds for tolerable Soviet behavior are conceivable and desirable, how Great Power bilateralism contributes to a Western constraints policy, what the likely Soviet incentives for maintaining a cautious political posture might be and which elements of a Western constraints policy seem identifiable at the present state.

SHIFTING SOVIET PRIORITIES

Soviet anxiety not to destabilize or delegitimize political control is likely to remain the number one priority within any Soviet framework, even though in practical terms this may be more important in relatively stalemated and *static* situations such as most of the stalemated Europeon scene of the 1950s and 1960s than in more open-ended *dynamic* ones as they seem to have developed in the 1970s. We may, indeed, be witnessing a political process in Europe that Soviet leaders could increasingly consider to be sufficiently fluid to feel less constrained by intra-systemic requirements for stability. This prospect calls for a closer study of possible projections of Soviet military power and potential crises where the application of Soviet military power could make all the difference, and for an assessment of the uses of Soviet military power within what is likely to be the political framework for Soviet crisis decision-making.

In the world that has emerged since the late 1940s, static East-West situations have been characterized by threats of instant and multilateral responses (so-called "indivisibility of defense"), which tended to be generalized into political opportunity costs and military risks of major Soviet incursions anywhere. The tendency of static situations to reinforce themselves, plus a Western propensity to disregard long-term perspectives in times of relative stability have led Western foreign policy elites to believe that, in addition to requirements for intrasystemic stability, deterrence by military force-matching is the only other major constraint that determines Soviet military behavior. However, while force-matching will continue to be important in any East-West context for the foreseeable future, Soviet leaders presumably have never viewed deterrence as an isolated condition, and recurrent failures in the West to recognize the political nature of Soviet approaches to the West may well have induced policies of over-reliance on military deterrence. Such over-reliance helped to destabilize political regimes and relations in the West up to a point where domestically comfortable deterrence postures may no longer be sufficient, because application of military power and the need to check this in real conflict situations seems much more conceivable now than, say, ten years ago.

The dynamic and politically fluid situations that may emerge in Western Europe may be more conducive to selective Soviet approaches that could involve even the application of military power. Selective Soviet campaigns would be less likely than in static conditions to have repercussions on Soviet political control within the Soviet orbit. Up to the present détente policies are undoubtedly competitive games for mutual influence, where the Soviet Union (with the possible exception of Angola) has thus far refrained cautiously from maximum exploitations of crises in the West or conflicts affecting the West. But European or related contingencies are conceivable that will confront Soviet leaders with policy choices where it may be hard to assess whether a more erratic approach is worth potential setbacks elsewhere or will be consistent with more cooperative approaches in other areas. Soviet behavior in the early days of the October War suggested to many Western observers a readiness to switch policies rapidly if the need arises; it should be added, however, that it also eventually demonstrated high priority for preserving great power bilateralism.

As such policy choices become more likely, comparative advantages and risks for Soviet moves in the West will become the most important factor governing constraints on Soviet military behavior for most practical purposes, even though doctrinally intrasystemic stability will continue to be the first priority. The more Western Europe is dominated by Social-democratism, the more Soviet leaders will be concerned over potential feedback within the Soviet orbit. The immediate post-war lessons of 1945-47 are likely to be very much alive in Soviet minds, but the enormous differences in Soviet potentials then and now are hardly less impressive. Thus for Western analysts it is of paramount interest to assess potential Soviet crisis calculations in terms of relative advantages and opportunity costs outside the Soviet orbit. Soviet relations with the U.S. are naturally of utmost concern in any such effort. The issue of such major policy choices will rank prominently in current Soviet policy formation; however, at this stage, it seems undecided whether the outcome will tend to contain Soviet behavior in the late 1970s and possibly beyond, or whether it will encourage more erratic behavior.

THE EUROPEAN CONTEXT OF BIG TWOISM

This chapter sets out to assess whether and to what extent relations with the United States are likely to be conducive to cautious and constrained Soviet military behavior. It is confined to Soviet military behavior in Europe. This is not to say, however, that useful lessons cannot be drawn from Soviet behavior in other regions. In fact, the eventual collapse in Southeast Asia or the Soviet role in Angola seems to have generated generalized impressions among leading West European politicians, as well as observers. In spite of a number of consistent beliefs and increasing capabilities to project power on a global scale, Soviet policies are unlikely to be continuously knit together on the basis of some global master plan. Soviet behavior along the Soviet perimeter, however, presumably *is* conceived in a geopolitical perspective that provides some coherence. There is also a steady expansion of Soviet logistic infrastructures and networks of military cooperation that seems to follow a limited set of patterns. Moreover, Soviet leaders are most certainly aware of possible spill-overs from one region to another; Korea in the early 1950s, and Vietnam in the late 1960s and beyond, provided lessons of sorts. But in spite of all this, Soviet diplomacy is characterized by a strong tendency toward regionalization and the establishment of multilateral frameworks of cooperation that promise Soviet dominance—at least in the long run. Except for sweeping solutions (like gaining political control over Western Europe's Middle East oil resources), this regionalist approach thus has to reckon with conditions and forces in any given region. Obviously this is bound to affect uniformities of means and tactics.

More important, the respective roles of the two great powers have a number of specific characteristics in Europe that determine their relationships to a considerable degree. History since 1945 provides abundant evidence. The two great powers may in fact turn out to be more competitive in other regions, and Russian-American competitive drives in the Pacific in the nineteenth century already pointed in such directions. But unlike any other regional superpower competition, major changes in the respective roles of the two great powers in Europe are likely to have considerable feedback into Soviet and/or American society.

There exists a longstanding Franco-German tradition of prophecies about the emerging two great powers and the ways these are going to affect the fate of Europe. Friedrich von List and Alexis Charles de Tocqueville, Constantin Frantz and Henri Martin are parallel in their early anticipation of Russia's and the United States' role in Europe. In many ways their global perspectives even today improve our understanding of European power relations—except for those modern realities like nuclear weapons that induced narrowly conceived views of the contemporary European scene, and yet played a decisive role that nobody could have anticipated, even during World War II, when the traditional European order finally broke down and the two great powers eventually dominated Europe.*

Those early visions of the two emerging great powers on the European scene, however inappropriate contemporary European observers may view them, obviously reflect a historical development that is still present in most of the current integrationist concepts as well as many philosophical concerns over Europe's steady decline. History as well as the basic interests of the two great powers attach particular importance to Europe as the most crucial area of their future interactions.

So while Europeans have every reason not to become confined to an essentially regionalist framework of foreign policy-making, they should remain equally aware of the fact that the European engagement of the two great powers has unique characteristics. For all practical purposes their dominant roles in Europe are permanent conditions, even though possible combinations of American temporary indifference to what is at stake and higher Soviet risk-taking efforts to capitalize upon European weaknesses could well change political power structures in the foreseeable future. Most observers today agree that an American threat to intervene in Europe in the early stages of World War II would have constrained Hitler decisively, but even after Pearl Harbor, Roosevelt had to wait for Hitler's declaration of war in order to intervene politically in Europe. There is an American propensity to be politically restrained too long, with the consequence of then having to use military force excessively. With U.S. forces deployed in Western Europe, the situation may be altogether different, but American self-paralysis is something Soviet planners may realistically consider even in European contingencies.

---

* Not surprisingly, many of these early anticipations occurred when the Holy Alliance began to disintegrate, but there are even some earlier ones. To quote Baron Melchior von Grimm, a diplomat of German origin, who lived in Paris as Catherine II's emissary: "Two empires will then share all the advantages of civilization, of the power of genius, of letters, of arts, of arms and industry: Russia on the eastern side and America . . . on the western side, and we other peoples of the nucleus will be too degraded, too debased, to know otherwise than by a vague and stupid tradition what we have been." (31 December 1790).

SHADOWS OF MILITARY POWER:
TYPES OF POSSIBLE CONTINGENCIES

Given European trends as well as the possibility of American inaction, a number of types of contingencies can be distinguished where the Soviet Union might in fact consider the application of military power, although this could happen in a wide variety of ways, with overt aggression being the least likely case. It should be noted, however, that in order to be able to constrain Soviet military behavior in European crisis contingencies, considering major overt aggression is one way of reckoning with available escalatory potentials which will weigh heavily in any such cases.

In addition to potential crises inside the Soviet orbit which are unlikely to trigger U.S. responses on a priori grounds, there are essentially four types of contingencies:

1. Violent domestic crises in West European countries, e.g., as a result of forceful leftist takeovers or as forceful attempts to keep leftist governments in power, in spite of different election outcomes: In addition to non-military Soviet help, the Soviet Union could reply positively to pro-Soviet political forces that ask for Soviet intervention, or it might make non-military help dependent on granting base rights for Soviet military forces, thus cementing Soviet control in these respective countries, or it might threaten to intervene and make such threats visible by maneuvers in appropriate areas.
2. Military conflicts between West European countries (as was almost the case between Greece and Turkey over Cyprus), where the Soviet Union could get involved in a number of ways. (In the absence of a powerful figure like Karamanlis, the last conflict over Cyprus could well have deteriorated so as to stir anti-Americanism in Greece even further, while at the same time escalating into open military conflict with Turkey. Given Turkish military superiority, Soviet help might conceivably have appeared as a last resort to Greek leaders.)
3. Domestic crises in grey area countries like Yugoslavia where a threat of more direct Soviet military involvement is conceivable in a variety of ways. Whatever the relevancy status of the so-called "Polarka Plan" may be today or in fact was in 1968, it certainly shed some light on the ways Central Europe could be affected by any such contingency. (This plan was a Soviet contingency for invading Austria and Yugoslavia as reported by General Sejna, a Czechoslovakian defector in 1968.)

4. Spill-over from Middle East crises. The application of Soviet military force is conceivable in at least four different ways. There could be a Soviet takeover, say, in Iran, in the context of a succession crisis or in the context of a subregional military conflict where the Soviet Union chooses to assist "the other side"; there could be a request for Soviet military help in a domestic or subregional conflict in the area or, in fact, a Soviet assumption that help is being requested, with subsequent Soviet military action in the area; there could be a perceived threat of Western or specifically American intervention in the area which could trigger Soviet decisions to assist the Arabs, e.g., by considering Soviet action at vulnerable spots in Europe (Berlin); and there could be situations where the Soviet Union simply takes advantage of the consequences of Arab oil embargoes in Europe.

None of these contingencies may ever happen, but they could, and thus deserve consideration in major Western capitals. It is precisely with regard to such contingencies that the issue of constraints on Soviet military behavior in future European developments arise. It is obvious that in all four types of contingencies the U.S. role in Europe is directly affected. Thus the state of great power bilateralism in a given situation may well make all the difference.

THRESHOLDS AND CONSTRAINTS IN EUROPEAN CONTINGENCIES

Constraints on Soviet military behavior can refer to a variety of means and maneuvers other than the use of force or the explicit threat to use force. The very availability and deployment structure of Soviet forces can help to shape political relations in terms of what they deny or how they are being perceived (the "shadows of power"). Moreover, moving forces within the Soviet orbit could display ambiguities that could well be taken in the West as signals of Soviet determination without passing the threshold of overt commitment to act militarily (Soviet troop movements during the October War inside the Warsaw Treaty Organization (WTO) area may give some indications).

Constraints on such projections of military power are conceivable only as negotiating outcomes (substantial force reductions and severe movement constraints), which would obviously require substantial reciprocal concessions that might well offset possible advantages of constraints on Soviet military behavior. In any case, NATO certainly did not put much emphasis on constraints in Mutual Balanced Force Reduction (MBFR) negotiations and thus avoided the only potentially meaningful negotiating strategy.

It is difficult to see how the United States could check these potential projections of military power. Certainly maintaining their military presence in Europe is imperative; but even if U.S. forces in Europe remain more or less unchanged, it is the political decision-making power in Washington and the way it is perceived in Western Europe as well as in the Soviet Union that will make all the difference, and certainly American decisiveness cannot be taken for granted.

Constraints always are related to political thresholds, particularly those that result from influences of Western policies. While thresholds for military posturing can be fixed only by some kind of agreement which would have to be violated (like movement constraints), the threshold for military overt aggression is spelled out unilaterally by defense treaties and military preparation. In either case there is, of course, enough room for ambiguities. Between shows of military posturing—deployment and movement—on the one hand, and overt aggression on the other, there is a wide variety of possible military moves with relatively low degrees of identifiability or visible commitment, such as military aid, actions by proxies, volunteers, and cut-offs, which may be most appropriate in the four nonclassical types of contingencies.

It is in the grey area between posturing and overt aggression that it is most difficult to establish thresholds: Agreements with the Soviet Union are as unlikely as is Alliance-consensus, and even if in one way or the other multilateral consensus would emerge, its unavoidable ambiguity as well as the differential political interests in any given conflict situation would make it very difficult to identify any violations so as to trigger appropriate responses. In fact, one intrinsic difficulty is that the way political resolve might be demonstrated would be extremely dependent on unpredictable circumstances and third party behavior. On the part of the more potent Western powers (i.e., at least the United States) it could turn out to be over- as well as under-reaction. A look at U.S. options in a Portuguese contingency prior to 15 November 1975 indicates how little opportunity there may exist for prudent response (e.g., to Soviet efforts to exploit the then pending Polish-Portuguese agreement on fishery and harbor facilities). But given Soviet options, the capability to respond to or incentives to restrain Soviet behavior are clearly needed.

In the past U.S. declaratory policies in terms of presidential doctrines served this purpose—most importantly the Truman Doctrine. This may not be a good time for any American president to issue another presidential doctrine or even to reinvigorate old ones. But while this may be regrettable, some kind of threshold ought to be spelled out for all four categories. In the Portuguese case the threshold might well be Soviet military access to Portugal in terms of base rights and facilities, i.e., it should be clear to the Soviet Union as well as to other countries involved that this would be considered as violating vital interests, and any further pursuance would run military risks. This was, in fact, part of Kissinger's otherwise ill-advised policy on Portugal.[1] Such a declaratory policy would make less likely spasm responses to political changes that could trigger off much worse consequences in other West-European countries. It would also reduce the risks of misjudgment on the part of the Soviet Union or potentially "responsive" forces in Western Europe or the Middle East. On the other hand, Kissinger's declaratory policy on the Soviet employment in Angola demonstrates how easily bluffs can be called.

While it is obvious that no such vital-interest doctrine can be translated into formal Alliance consensus, it is equally obvious that West European interests are profoundly at stake. This is particularly true in the West German case where deployment policies could increasingly become affected by requirements for mobility which West Germany might consider to be inconsistent with both its vital interests and the agreements on which the stationing of U.S. forces in Germany is based. On the other hand, not responding to such needs should they arise would probably be even more counterproductive than say Congressional action in order to cut off military aid to Turkey because an American law was violated that ruled out use of American arms among "friendly" nations. Thus the issue of declaratory policies on vital interests is bound to come up in West European capitals—both in terms of political thresholds and of appropriate responses. Otherwise potential applications of Soviet military power could go unchecked or potential American responses could turn out to be erratic.

CONDITIONS OF SOVIET MILITARY BEHAVIOR

There is a difference between political worst-case analyses and predictions. As Soviet policy choices emerge Soviet leaders may well decide not to go for "unintended expansion" or not to apply military force inasmuch as they

[1] cf. Tad Szulc, "Lisbon and Washington: Behind Portugal's Revolution." *Foreign Policy*, Winter 1975-76, No. 21, pp. 13-62.

expect similar or better outcomes without doing so; these could conceivably be Soviet preferences independent of what military risks Soviet leaders would otherwise expect to incur. Thus the notion of constraints does not imply that pressure to use or to threaten the use of military power would have to be strong in their absence. In order to anticipate likely frameworks of Soviet decision-making in a given crisis situation, it seems appropriate to consider Soviet military behavior in terms of a set of specifiable conditions that have to be fulfilled in a given situation in order for the application of military power for political purposes to be more likely. History as well as Soviet interest offers clues for attempts to specify such conditions, some of which are endemic while others may be susceptible to Western policy influences. Soviet military power may not be likely to be used for territorial gains, strategic improvements, or demonstrative campaigns, unless this occurs along with an effort to establish or consolidate political control in a way which promises good chances to isolate the country involved, to keep population and value damage low, to prevent the U.S. from getting involved militarily, and that moreover does not foreclose the chances of postwar recognition as well as political penetration of the Western rump. If this assessment is realistic, it seems that constraints in the sense of Western policy impacts on Soviet crisis decision-making to some degree can be designed so as to affect Soviet expectations and Soviet readiness to apply military power.

Establishing political thresholds other than agreed movement constraints and force ceilings on the one hand and defense doctrines on the other seems to be a prime prerequisite. Constraining Soviet escalatory potentials by force-matching, then, is a further necessary condition, but it is far from being a sufficient one, since in those non-classical types of contingencies the political capacity of Western countries to act is even more unpredictable than in a situation of overt Soviet aggression. Thus non-military constraints will weigh heavily; i.e., the risks of reducing political responsiveness to Soviet policy and political penetration elsewhere in the West, of reducing Western cooperation in Soviet modernization programs, or of feedbacks of reversed policies toward the West within the Soviet power structure. (For example, the consolidating effects of continued exposure in détente endeavors—"personalization"—could discontinue, or as in the Shelepin case disastrous exposure could help to destroy the domestic power base. Moreover, to the extent continued détente processes are likely to relativize the dominant role of the Soviet military apparatus, by both denying traditional roles and providing new ones, irreversibility of these processes could be a high stake of the political leadership.)

Non-military constraints can be of two kinds. They can involve a specific Western political commitment to create unproportional risks for the Soviet Union—defined in terms of vital interests and thresholds of political tolerance, but without specifying military means and responses. Or else, they can operate simply as perceived risks or penalties whatever Western political postures and declaratory policies may appear to be in a given situation. One could thus distinguish political and material non-military constraints.

Material constraints relate essentially to three types of interests: (1) gaining advantages, (2) establishing procedures, and (3) creating political conditions. Advantages could be temporary (like getting technological "know-how") or even *uno actu* (like gaining recognition of the status quo) even though some would have a more lasting character (like strategic parity as recognized through SALT agreements). Procedures (e.g., a multilateral framework for East-West consultation in Europe, or bilateralist approaches such as the cosponsored Security Council Resolutions 338, 339, and 340) may be of a more lasting nature, but they are not ends in themselves. Political conditions are expected to affect political behaviors in Europe so as to induce and reinforce new and lasting political structures. Discontinuing processes that would promise political conditions favorable from a Soviet point of view is likely to be the most important of these three possible concerns.

THE FRAMEWORK OF EXTERNAL ENGAGEMENTS

Soviet shifts in emphasis from one bilaterialist détente policy to another or from bilateralism to multilateralism and vice versa do not seem to occur accidentally, even though they are emerging as responses to opportunities rather than preplanned moves. But no tactical maneuvering is likely to blur the fact that relations with the United States are most crucial in Soviet Westpolitik. The role of the U.S. is crucial in regard to military constraints (deterrence) and political commitments (thresholds of tolerance) as well as to material constraints that emerge from improved political relations with the U.S. Both bipolarity based on retaliatory power and bilateralism resulting from cooperative political postures are important aspects of Soviet-American relations. Obviously the relative importance of these two elements is changing over time, and both the U.S. and the Soviet Union are likely not only to weigh them differently, but to try maneuvering the other side into accepting shifts in priority.

Soviet diplomacy is thus certain not to miss opportunities to induce changes in American foreign policy so as to strengthen the cooperative elements to the detriment of the retaliatory element. From a Soviet point of view, cooperative Great Power relations are desirable under almost any circumstances, but paradoxically they are not an end in themselves. If U.S.-Soviet relations could be assessed in isolation, bipolarity as well as bilateralism would lose its operational significance in Soviet policies quite dramatically. There would be only remotely conceivable pretexts for retaliatory measures in a bilateralist framework,* and cooperation would be confined to economic trade-offs and their potential spill-overs into societal structures.** The only exception to this rule would be in a situation where the "correlation of forces" is dramatically changed so as to deprive the U.S. of its "intermediary zones," as the jargon of Soviet political strategy occasionally puts it. Unlike American isolationists, Soviet planners seem to be aware of the likely impact the loss of the United States intermediary zones would have on Soviet-American relations and, in fact, on the inner fabric of American society.

Isolationists fail to recognize this truism. The most articulate and tough-minded among them (like Kenneth Waltz) would argue that the U.S. has the material power to sustain any repercussions of autarchy and isolation, but it is the political will and effective organization to generate and project power that will be affected.

There are two kinds of isolationism: One focuses on external involve-

---

* Presumably the Soviet Union was less concerned about American strategic superiority in the 1960s than in the 1950s: American ICBM and SLBM vastly increased Soviet vulnerability in terms of destructiveness and defenselessness, but U.S. bomber superiority in the 1950s was tied to unsatisfied political interests in Europe which from a Soviet point of view could conceivably have led into military conflict, whereas in the 1960s the division of Europe happened to lose its crucial character along with the U.S. missile build-up.

** It is worth mentioning, however, that trade and similar cooperative ventures have traditionally taken on symbolic value and operational instrumentality in relations between Russia and the United States. At a time when European countries refrained from recognizing the young American republic out of fear of British retaliation, St. Petersburg considered a trade agreement with Washington as a possible substitute in much the same way Washington was inclined to use trade agreements with the Soviet Union in recent decades.

ments, the other on internal repercussions of international change. While controlling and reducing foreign involvements seems to be the overriding concern in recent isolationist pledges, it is really the control of internal repercussions that will be crucial in the long run. To the extent the American Alliance system from the early 1950s into the late 1960s allowed to control interactions of American society with its international environment and, in fact, to keep it on a low level, it could well be called "extended isolationism." Obviously Vietnam not only showed the limits of this system, it tended to blur the distinction between controlling involvements and controlling repercussions altogether. Given the atypical character of the Vietnam involvement, it remains to be seen to what extent the American public will be aware of the risks of losing political control in other intermediary zones—above all Western Europe.

It is thus in the framework of external engagements of the two Great Powers that bipolarity and bilateralism display their full practical importance. It is the very power hard-line isolationists are counting on which makes external engagements unavoidable: There is no way to confine it within national borders. But more importantly, in view of potential long-term instabilities, it is in both superpowers' profound interest to control intermediary zones, even though this could conceivably take on forms other than that of military alliances. It is political control that matters. Whatever the perceived characteristics of the competitive U.S.-Soviet relationship, the balance of mutual political influence will be decisively determined by outcomes in crucial intermediary zones—above all in Western Europe. For too long the importance of Western Europe for the U.S. has been viewed in terms of maintaining or reducing American force levels. Important though the military posture is, concerns over its potential deterioration have tended to tolerate political conditions in some West European countries in ways which were bound to create domestic situations that are so much less manageable than the loss of a base or the withdrawal of a military contingent.

The outcome in Western Europe will depend heavily on the political will to maintain nondictatorial political regimes. There is no substitute for it. But it will equally depend on the political and economic backing of the United States. As Henry A. Kissinger put it recently: "It is left to the United States because fate has put us in a position where we are the only non-Communist country that is strong enough and domestically cohesive enough to play a world role. Therefore, if certain things are not done by us, they will not be done by anyone. And while it may be fairer if somebody else took some of the responsibility, the fact is that a catastrophe is no less real for having been brought about by attempts to shift responsibility to others." In other words, there is no substitute for an American political engagement either. Moreover, it is not only for the protection of the existing Western European political order, it is profoundly in the interest of maintaining the long-term stability of the American republic itself.

SOVIET STAKES IN BIG TWOISM

Obviously American and Soviet interests in intermediary zones—notably in highly industrialized areas like Western Europe—are quite asymmetrical. While the maintenance of liberal conditions in Western industrialized nations requires that both the U.S. and her partners recognize the vital importance of political engagements of the U.S. in crucial areas as a permanent condition, it is clearly in the Soviet interest to encourage domestic processes in those areas which tend to reduce American influence and increase Soviet leverage. (Soviet reluctance to press for an American pullout from Europe has often been misread in the West as evidencing Soviet readiness to accept a long-term presence of the U.S. in Europe and the kind of stability that is expected in the West to result from an American military engagement.)

Given the crucial importance of intermediary zones as a framework for Big Twoism, this reflects the very ambiguity of Soviet-American relations. From a Soviet point of view Big Twoism itself is but a transitory condition. At the same time, however, cooperative relations with the U.S. at the present stage of international development are necessary for any promising Soviet political strategy. Moreover, it is in the Soviet interest to develop the bilateralist features of Soviet-American relations to the extent possible, precisely because of the nature of great power competition over influence in intermediary zones.

Soviet interests in Soviet-American bilateralism are, of course, complex. Without providing a full catalog, Soviet interests can be seen on five different levels, i.e., with regard to internal payoffs, the international status of the Soviet Union, regionally unspecified international advantages, influencing West European processes, and reinforcing the domestic base for bilateralism within the U.S.

Internal payoffs—i.e., within the Soviet orbit—are those affecting legit-

²Interview with Secretary of State Henry Kissinger, in *U.S. News and World Report*, June 23, 1975, p. 27.

imacy and modernization. They were certainly high on the Soviet agenda after the new Soviet Westpolitik had eventually emerged in the spring of 1971. While both legitimacy and modernization called for cooperation with Western Europe and Japan as well, only American consent could deliver the kind of acceptance of the status quo Moscow was driving at and only the American economy had promising technological know-how, financial capacity and a readiness to carry the vast development projects in Siberia that the ninth Five-Year Plan was calling for.

In both regards, however, returns were likely to be diminishing. While the internal need for legitimacy is a perennial one in the Soviet system (as in any other, even though with fewer means for continuous supply) specific measures of acceptance by the West can hardly be withdrawn and can thus be delivered but once. Given the calculated ambiguities in détente outcomes like the Berlin agreement, Moscow presumably was anxious to consume Western supplied legitimacy within as short a period as possible. Soviet pressure for an early summit level conclusion of the CSCE is but one indication. Modernization, on the other hand, may well have appealed to Moscow as a longer-term objective, not only in terms of internal payoffs, but potentially in terms of increasing Soviet leverage over Western and notably the American economy as well. Integrating the Soviet Union into the Western world trade and monetary systems has been among the ultimate goals of American détente policy since 1971 as a means toward "domesticizing" the Soviet Union. Moscow is likely to have pursued economic cooperation with a view toward becoming capable of manipulating American (and other Western) price levels for important commodities like agricultural products or gasoline, of influencing the American labor market and of creating strategically crucial dependencies on Soviet controlled energy supply. Both political strategists for the time being are little more than wishful thinking, but their fundamental difference and, indeed, competitive relationship deserves to be kept in mind. At some stage this very competition may after all become unavoidable in one way, or another. But while the Soviet interest in U.S. technology may persist for some years to come, other economic incentives may be considerably less now than they were in 1971. The increase in oil and gold pieces, good harvests first and the obvious separability of grain deals from other issues of Soviet-American bilateralism later, increasing awareness of potential feedbacks of cooperative ventures within the Soviet economic planning system—all have worked in the same direction, as the somewhat unexpected political reluctance in the West and above all in the United States to get engaged on a large scale. There still is a discernible Soviet interest—but much less so than a few years ago, even though at this stage Soviet emphasis on economic cooperation could still go either way.

Like legitimacy, enhancing the international status of the Soviet Union in part had to be acquired through Western recognition. There is a wide variety of means, to be sure, ranging from a growing capability to project military power on a global scale to efforts of legalistic engineering in order to see favorable regionally applied principles of interstate relations accepted, as is evidenced by current Soviet obsessions over the hegemony clause in the impending agreement between Japan and China. While enhancing international status is a long-term goal, Western recognition is important only during a transitory phase. Like legitimacy, international status cannot effectively be renounced. But during the present phase of international development, it still seems to be high on the Soviet agenda.

In many ways parity with the United States and nondiscrimination by the United States were most important parts of this Soviet drive. There are embryonic forms of this in institutions like the Soviet-American co-chairmanship within the Geneva disarmament talks (Conference of the Committee on Disarmament) or in the joint Soviet-American draft of the nonproliferation treaty in the spring of 1967. It became manifest in the Moscow agreement on "Basic Principles" in May 1972 governing great power behavior. Similar agreements on principles had been concluded with other nations, to be sure; agreements with France, Turkey, and above all the Moscow agreement with West Germany preceded it and so did the Shanghai Communiqué. But obviously the 1972 agreement with Washington was considered most important in Moscow, and it was considered the most important of all Soviet-American agreements. SALT I consecrated strategic parity and thus implemented the agreement on principles. A Most Favored Nation status for the Soviet Union was above all seen as another way of enhancing status. In order to gain American recognition of the Soviet Union as the second world power, Moscow had to first acquire most of the attributes unilaterally. Nevertheless acceptance by the United States and the perception of this by third parties was considered so important by Moscow that Soviet leadership refrained from any attempt to exploit the domestic crisis over Watergate or, on a somewhat lower level, canceled the trade agreement only when the low credit levels offered by the U.S. made it virtually impossible for the Soviet leadership to justify any other outcome. But while here too the realities of Big Twoism were crucial from a Soviet point of view,

Moscow may soon see its position sufficiently strengthened internationally so as to no longer pay a price for status recognition. It is likely to be a transitory goal.

Unlike acquiring international status through Western and notably American recognition, improving conditions for expanding Soviet political influence in unspecified areas is a less irreversible, but also a longer-lasting process. It is likely to be affected by the very ambivalence of Soviet-American relations—competitiveness as well as Big Twoism. But a number of likely consequences of blossoming Big Twoism can be listed. It will favor more it will raise the political threshold for hostile reactions of third parties toward friendly foreign policy orientations of third parties toward the Soviet Union; Soviet moves such as political support of communist drives in Western Europe or expansion of the Soviet military infrastructure outside the Soviet orbit (e.g., in Somali); it tends to regionalize patterns of Western influence; it reinforces pluralism in Western foreign policy making by widening the range of perceived options and diversifying foreign policy elites; it enhances the prospects for political penetration of domestic bodies politic as well as for economic dependence on Soviet cooperativeness; it discourages Western defense spending and intelligence operations. All these are but likely trends which Soviet planners could reasonably expect even though none is certain to have outcomes favorable to the Soviet Union. The role of Big Twoism may, in fact, be somewhat intangible.

Whether or not Big Twoism is having more lasting effects in intermediary zones so as to turn tactical Soviet considerations into strategic ones is a matter of political conditions at a given stage of development and of the dynamics of political processes within given regional or domestic frameworks. If leftist political trends in a number of West European countries continue, the Soviet leadership could well decide that "irreversibility" of the process has become a plausible objective that deserves a high price if necessary. In this perspective Big Twoism could well be seen as affecting political conditions in Western Europe more profoundly than in some other intermediary zones—even today. It deprives Western Europe of integrative options considered to be hostile. An "Atlantic option" as conceived in the early 1960s in terms of nuclear participation would appear to be incompatible with Big Twoism, and a "European option" involving a nuclear weapons capability would be rendered infeasible by reinforced pluralism in foreign policy making in all West European nations—except for the technological support needed in order to set up a militarily useful force which again would be incompatible with Big Twoism, to mention just one condition. Major West European countries may, in fact, see incentives not to fall behind the United States in cooperative ventures with the Soviet Union, as was the case for example when Washington was driving toward an MBFR agreement and some West European countries somewhat perversely were anxious to get indigenous forces included in order to minimize the impact of Soviet-American bilateralism. In much more subtle ways West Germany's Ostpolitik was in part an effort to preempt dire consequences of growing Soviet-American consent to deblock their relations by eliminating the stalemating mechanisms resulting from the German issue.

Since political conservatism rightly or wrongly has tended to focus on either the "Atlantic" or the "European" option and has given relatively low priority to cooperative relations with the Soviet Union, Big Twoism is above all likely to reinforce leftist and neutralist trends in most, if not all, West European countries. However, these trends exist in any case and on the other hand, some degree of cooperation between the two great powers is considered desirable today also by most conservative political forces. But while political conservatism may have lost some of its traditional vulnerabilities which resulted from the nature of the stalemating system of East-West relations in Europe in the 1950s and well into the 1960s, it has yet to redefine its purpose so as to participate again in the shaping of future political structures in Western Europe. From a Soviet point of view, Soviet-American bilateralism and its very visibility by West European electorates is one of the most important political conditions for influencing domestic and regional processes in Western Europe that are favorable to the Soviet Union—at least so long as the American political role in Western Europe is not dramatically reduced or anti-Americanism in Western Europe is not much stronger.

This is not to say that Soviet-American bilateralism is undesirable from a West European point of view. It is a political challenge to existing liberal conditions which has yet to find its response. Moreover, it is unavoidable anyway. And it is undoubtedly not altogether a Soviet success story as changes of respective roles and influences in the Middle East since the first summit in Moscow in May 1972 demonstrates—and this in an area crucially important to Western Europe. As Henry Kissinger put it, it is equally "a means of controlling the conflict with the Soviet Union."[3]

It can be safely assumed that the Soviet leadership is anxious to pursue Soviet-American bilateralism so as to turn it into a process that promises

[3]Ibid., Interview in *U.S. News and World Report, loc. cit.,* p. 22.

irreversibility, even though some of the Soviet interests are only transitory in nature, or at least make sense operationally only within narrow time horizons.

However, Big Twoism is constantly threatened by immobility because the range of cooperative options is fairly narrow; at times it has been kept alive through gimmickry in very much the same way as the Atlantic Alliance was in earlier years. Continued normalization of U.S.-Soviet relations is likely to put into proper perspective that there are only so many things the Soviet Union can deliver in order to fuel bilateralism. More specifically, the American public seems to be quite sensitive toward potential Soviet leverage in U.S. domestic affairs: (1) concerns arose that the grain deals were possible factors causing considerable price increases in the American agricultural market; (2) Congressional response to the Mayaguez incident and the voting on defense spending, in an era which otherwise is characterized by a low degree of bipartisanship, seem to indicate a need to reassert throughout the government a capacity to respond to international challenges; and (3) the continued increase of American influence in the Middle East could, in fact, justify American confidence in present developments as echoed by Secretary Kissinger's assessments that "the essential architecture of our foreign policy is sound and will be sound." The fact that it has survived some of the shocks of this past year proves that it is sound.[4] But while these limits, as seen from a Soviet point of view, all exist, it seems to be equally true that the political changeability of present Soviet-American relations toward a less cooperative posture is remote. It is part of the "essential architecture," not only in regard to American diplomacy, but to American domestic politics as well. On the other hand, recent votes on defense matters are far from signalling a growing readiness to become committed to new kinds of defense cooperation that could affect the Soviet Union, even though the letter of 76 Senators in support of Israel indicates that a potential for more than just reacting to crises as they emerge does exist.

CONCLUSION: SOME ELEMENTS OF A WESTERN CONSTRAINT POLICY

Given this variety of Soviet interests in continued Great Power bilateralism, it can be said that Soviet political strategy above all has tried to turn political processes in Western Europe and in the United States into what

4Ibid., Interview in *U.S. News and World Report, loc. cit.*, p. 27.

might look increasingly susceptible to Soviet penetration. Extending political control as the result of favorable political processes is the very essence of Soviet Westpolitik.[5] There can be little doubt that the Soviet approach is generally cautious and that the deep-rooted confidence in favorable changes in the "correlation of forces" makes deliberate use of military force in order to extend influence a rather remote possibility. Even though the shadows of military power may be expected, and indeed may help to reinforce processes in Moscow's favor, the Soviet Union is, "peaceful." It may not be reassuring that the Soviet Union is unlikely to use its military power because it hopes to achieve similar or better outcomes without. But since the Soviet Union does not really have an alternative to competitive cooperation either, it is a challenge that can be met. This is why a Western policy designed to constrain Soviet military behavior is not pointless. It is not the hard core of what a Western approach to the Soviet challenge ought to be because it has to cope above all with a political rather than a military threat, but it can establish boundaries for tolerable political developments in Western Europe.

There are, to be sure, inherent instabilities in the European situation which neither side may be able to control sufficiently. Four types of crises have been distinguished. In the absence of obvious constraints the Soviet leadership may even consider the use of military power in indirect ways rather than overtly. But under present circumstances the Soviet leadership is likely to refrain from any military engagement that might discontinue political processes toward socialism in Western Europe and Great Power bilateralism as one of the major conditions of those processes. The stakes in pursuing Great Power bilateralism are high and the risks of disrupting it in a crisis can be high also. It should be added, however, that Soviet interest in Big Twoism is a potential constraint on Soviet behavior only up to a point. The low changeability within the American body politic and the encapsulating effects resulting from either side's interest in keeping a crisis under control may well turn out to leave Great Power bilateralism compatible with a variety of potential crisis situations.

Bilateralism is likely to be a strong material constraint if there is a perceived incompatibility in the Soviet perspective. Then the threat of its discontinuance enters the balance of comparative risks and penalties, and will weigh heavily. In Angola this was obviously not the case. There is no way of

---

[5]For a fuller discussion in Uwe Nerlich, "NATO, EEC and the Politics of Détente," in Nils Andren and Karl E. Birnbaum, ed., *Beyond Détente: Prospects for East-West Cooperation and Security in Europe,* A.W. Sythoff, 1976.

spelling out in which circumstances Western approaches will be reversed unfavorably. But in the absence of any indication Moscow may expect the threshold to be high. After all, the Soviet intervention in the CSSR was barely enough to convince President Johnson that in the circumstances he had to cancel the impending summit. Perhaps on balance a discontinuance would weigh differently if at the same time the prospects for an American-West European regrouping during a crisis had disappeared, but for the time being a reinforced Alliance in the West with unpredictable domestic conse-quences is likely to be considered a high penalty in Moscow.

While there can hardly be a useful declaratory policy turning material into political constraints, the context of Western diplomacy may well make a difference. If vital interests were being defined with regard to the four types of crises and thresholds for tolerable action were to become visible for Soviet leaders, this by implication would make them more sensitive to the prospects of discontinuance. But this would require above all a somewhat coordinated Western approach to the various types of political conflict which might turn into open crisis. At this stage, this seems like asking too much. At the same time it necessitates an appropriate modernization of the mili-tary posture in Western Europe. The Soviet Union has continuously improved its military capability so as to back up political processes. NATO has always focused on major overt aggression and thus failed to provide the capabilities needed to cope with limited crisis situations. Whether or not there will emerge the political will to modernize military forces in Western Europe so as to provide useful means of influencing outcomes of crisis situations remains to be seen.[6] It may well turn out to become a major test as to whether modernizing defense is considered compatible with Big Twoism in order to match its potential consequences in Western Europe. Major crises in Europe are more likely within the next ten years than within past decades. There is no substitute for American participation in such crisis management and reacting to such crises only as they emerge is almost certain to invite disaster.

[6]See Uwe Uwe Nerlich, "Continuity and Change: The Political Context of Western Europe's Defense," in Johan J. Holst and Uwe Nerlich, eds., *Beyond Nuclear Deterrence: New Aims, New Arms,* Crane, Russak, 1976.

Consequences for Western Foreign Policies of Future Applications of Soviet Military Power

KLAUS RITTER AND LAWRENCE L. WHETTEN

One of the most controversial single aspects of the East-West confrontation has been the accurate determination of Soviet military capabilities and political intentions. Indeed U.S. estimates of Soviet power and perceptions of Moscow's objectives in international crises have often been erroneous.[1] (Defense Secretary Robert McNamara told a confident American audience in 1965 that the Soviets had given up the strategic arms race and Secretary of State Kissinger admitted that Washington was completely surprised by the outbreak of the October War, made possible by Moscow's unexpected supply of "decisive" weapons to the Arabs.)[2]

These U.S. misperceptions have been attributed to a variety of reasons: (1) bureaucratic politics and interagency rivalry; (2) technological improvements in both surveillance techniques and weapons capabilities; (3) prevailing

[1] Albert Wohlstetter, "Is There a Strategic Arms Race?" *Foreign Policy*, Summer and Fall 1974.

[2] *USIS Bulletin*, No. 192, 15 October, and No. 200, 26 October 1973.

strategic doctrines at any given time; (4) the influence of arms control advocates who correlate weapons stockpiles with political tensions; and (5) the general understanding that under the threat of nuclear war military force would be employed in a discrete, responsible manner.[3] At critical junctures threat perceptions usually involve a degree of uncertainty, which require that subjective judgments must be introduced. When intuition must be substituted for hard intelligence, threat estimates become lowest common denominator compromises between contending organizations and various interest groups. Paradoxically, several additional factors provided both a hedge against misperceptions, but also contributed to inaccurate assessments: (1) the cohesion of the Western containment alliances; (2) Allied naval supremacy; (3) U.S. strategic superiority; and (4) American confidence that strategic thought with its own intrinsic "laws" was an exclusive U.S. domain with which other nations would sooner or later comply.

An underlying rationale reinforcing these asymmetrical Western advantages was that political leverage against the Soviet Union was difficult to correlate directly with strategic nuclear weapons. There was no danger in marginal increases in power because they could not be converted to political influence. Indeed political utility could best be extracted indirectly— by demonstrating restraint while maintaining a position of unquestioned strength. The argument of the lack of political convertability of strategic nuclear weapons was cited as the justification for finally relinquishing U.S. superiority.

The difficulty with such rationale was that it did not fall within the "scientifically-binding laws of strategy" governing Soviet defense planning. Moscow ignored the entire assumption and attached a high degree of political value to nuclear weapons and strategic forces. When technology and resources have been available, the Soviets have consistently invested in programs designed first to deter and then to match U.S. capabilities. Minimum deterrence force structures have been systematically upgraded and military parity has been a deliberately established goal.

Thus the U.S. misperceived not only Soviet technical and industrial capabilities to match U.S. force postures, but it also erroneously calculated the political utility Moscow attaches to strategic equality, especially among the newly contested third parties. The regional surveys included in the preceding chapters, indicate the linkage that the Soviets maintain between mili-

[3]Leon Sloss, "The U.S.-Soviet Military Balance: Changing American Perceptions," in Lawrence L. Whetten, ed., *The Future of Soviet Military Power*, Crane, Russak, 1976.

tary power and political influence. They have gone beyond the U.S. notion of the 1960s that political rewards could be earned by exercising restraint from a position of strength. The Soviets argue that the credibility of military power depends upon the willingness and ability to use force when it serves Moscow's interests.[4] They have now developed nuclear strategic forces that in some cases are quantitatively superior to their U.S. counterparts and limited long-range logistical and intervention capabilities.[4a] The upgrading of intervention capabilities was demonstrated in 1975-76 when Moscow successfully intervened in Angola; a similar operation in the Belgian Congo 15 years before had been effectively blocked by the U.S. Also in 1975 the USSR constructed a major basing complex in Somalia; similar efforts in Cuba five years earlier had been decisively challenged by Washington.

From a doctrinal viewpoint, the Soviets have apparently concluded that if military force has been effectively demonstrated, the imposition of subsequent constraints will be politically more persuasive. In other words, the old adage is still applicable: opponents must be convinced of the risks imparted by one's military capabilities if their threatened use is to have a persuasive political impact. It is from this position of enhanced strategic strength that Moscow can be expected to conduct a more flexible foreign policy that may, when necessary, include an increased willingness to accept risks when challenged or to be more assertive under either favorable or deteriorating political conditions.

In the technical sense, the Soviets have not achieved military superiority over the U.S. or the West; rather they have attained parity marked by disparities and persisting physical constraints, e.g., assured access to strategic oceans. More important, it has successfully used its military power to gain American recognition of its political equality with the United States,[5] which is now seen as probably the most important single achievement of the Brezhnev era. The very magnitude of this success underscores the importance, from the Soviet viewpoint, of strategic parity to political coexistence.

[4]cf. William F. Scott, *Soviet Sources of Military Doctrine and Strategy*, Crane, Russak, 1975; and General-Major A.S. Milovidov, ed., *Problems of Contemporary War*, 1972, U.S. Government Printing Office.

[4a]According to Helmut Sonnenfeldt, "The Soviet Union is only just beginning its truly 'imperial' phase. Its military forces have acquired intercontinental reach only fairly recently. Its capacity to influence forces in remote areas is of relatively recent standing. And it is only just acquiring the habit of defining its interests on a global rather than a solely continental basis." Interview, *International Herald Tribune*, 26 January 1976.

[5]Formally acknowledged in the November 1974 Vladivostok communiqué.

How, then, should Soviet military power be analyzed? At least four prime factors should be assessed. First is the conventional technique for measuring military balances, including weapons capabilities, logistics, training, fire power indicies, concepts of operation, mobility, modernization rates, manpower and material reserves, mobilization rates and support from alliances partners. There are few startling new methodological innovations on the horizon over those presently in use that will improve the assessments of military proficiency under various types of combat. Estimating the kill—probably of a given air defense system, for example, must include all components, ranging from weapons characteristics and reliability, to locations and mobility, to guidance and vulnerability to countermeasures, to resupply and support capability, to tactics finally and morale. Some of these physical factors are readily susceptible to surveillance and can be accurately measured; others are highly subjective and can at best be determined intuitively.

The second factor includes the entire system or network of perceptions about adversary political intention. The full spectrum encompasses the range of image projections, societal aspirations, political culture, geostratic components, traditional constraints and economic considerations. Relative accessability and complexity of the decision-making machinery contribute to the accuracy of analyses. The closed nature of the Soviet governmental process reduces knowledgeability about inputs in given decisions and confines assessment to observable outputs or policy actions. This limitation is balanced in part by the more complex U.S. political system that includes far more variables requiring broader expertise.

A third area for investigation is the overall stability of the international system and its susceptibility to arms competition and other destabilizing factors. The sources of tension and the chances of hostilities are the vital components of stability studies. But the types and nature of possible military contingencies must also be considered—fought by whom, against whom, and for what purposes.

A fourth factor also relates to systemic stability, namely crisis management. Before crises erupt careful study should be made in potential trouble spots of the ability of small states to influence events, the purposes, likelihood and means for great power involvement, the incentive that might be extended to induce to achieve a peaceful settlement, the types of coercion that might be employed, and the linkages between the respective national interests involved and those elsewhere that provide leverage against the various participants.[6] The purpose of such contingency planning is to provide insight into probable Soviet behavior and risk-taking patterns and into the nature of the levers of influence that can be employed to restore stability.

While all four factors are common-sense approaches, they are seldom viewed as methodological components of an overall assessment of Soviet military power.

PARITY AND SYSTEMIC DEVELOPMENT

Three main developments contributed to the degree of systemic stability presently known as the special great power relationship. The first was the nature of anticipated change in the system and its component or subsystems. Lenin's original injunctions about coexistence and the subsequent conduct of Soviet foreign policy was based on the fundamental assumption that the "correlation of historic forces" would eventually revolutionize the entire system, component by component.[7] The countervailing sweeping changes proposed by the West created the stalemate that characterized the Cold War. It was not until East-West relations began to destalemate in the 1960s that the prospects for realistic changes began to emerge. Paradoxically, frustrations over the respective designs for transformations of the system led to mutual acceptance of the central features of the status quo. This transition "from détente based on change to détente based on the status quo" led to the thaw in East-West relations.[8] In Willy Brandt's terms, the best way to change the status quo is to accept it and thus provide a framework for mutual accommodation.[9]

[6]For example, on 30 January, Secretary of State, Henry Kissinger, stated before the Senate Finance Committee that due to the Soviet involvement in Angola it would not be timely to extend U.S. commercial credits to the USSR.

[7]Khrushchev stated that peaceful coexistence was not a state of tranquility, but one of development and struggle. It presumes the revolutionary transformation of society that will accelerate the collapse of capitalism. Nikita S. Khrushchev, *For Victory in Peaceful Coexistence with Capitalism*, 1960.

[8]Pierre Hassner, *Europe in the Age of Negotiation*, The Washington Papers, No. 8, 1973.

[9]According to Egon Bahr the *Grundvertrag* clarifies the elements of "non-comparability" of the German states which have ceased to be obstacles to the normal contribution the German peoples can make to stability. This kind of "abnormal normalization is based on the mutual desire to cooperate, but also to maintain their respective distance. "German Ostpolitik and Superpower Relations." Speech delivered at Tutzing, FRG, 11 July 1973, reprinted in *Survival*, November-December 1973.

The second contributory factor to the special relationship was the change in political structures within both blocs. The most important changes have not occurred between the two camps, but rather within both. These changes were the products of indigenous conditions and external stimuli from East-West interactions.[10] Clearly the nature of the modifications within the two subsystems differed. In the East the principles and practice of democratic centralism and integration were reinforced under Soviet hegemony and in the West pluralism was reaffirmed and traditional conflicts were only partially muted. Both subsystems, however, also experienced the simultaneous broadening and narrowing of their foreign policy objectives. In the East the fissures created over the German problem generated individual, but orchestrated, efforts to settle national grievances with Bonn and to develop commercial contacts with the West. Yet the instruments of Soviet control were steadily strengthened. In the West, on the other hand, the *Ostverträge* were designed for wider and more varied relations with the East. Yet the multilateral negotiations at MBFR, CSCE, and the Common Market created renewed, and on some issues, unique solidarity within the pluralistic West. The broadening and narrowing of foreign policy aims created both the opportunities and reassurance necessary for the special relationship to function.

The third pillar of the special relationship was the Soviet achievement of strategic parity. As mentioned above parity with disparities is the underlying stabilizer in great power relations; indeed it has become the "equalizer" in the fragile balance between the world's most industrialized society and the leading developing nation. Of the three causal factors in détente, military parity is the most important; it is the most sensitive and susceptible to national security interests. It was not until the United States acknowledged Soviet strategic parity that the other two facors in the special relationship could reach fruition and that issues affecting vital national interests were finally raised for negotiations. The preservation of parity thus has become the "self-regulating" mechanism in the stability of the special relationship. Disparities and asymmetrics can reasonably be expected to be refined or off-set. But any unilaterally perceived "tilting" of the mechanism to one side or the other may reinforce a perceived threat by the adversary and possibly jeopardize the stability of the relationship. Firmer underpinnings for the relationship are desirable based upon greater understanding of individual political interests and mutually acceptable standards for great power behavior.

[10]Uwe Nerlich, "Beyond Détente: European East-West Relationships in Atlantic Perspective."

The relevance of parity and the correlation of military power to the political character of the special relationship has been expressed by Kissinger's chief adviser, Helmut Sonnenfeldt.

> It [U.S. détente policy] is an attempt to evolve a balance of incentives for positive behavior and penalties for belligerence; the objective being to instill in the minds of our potential adversaries an appreciation of the benefits of cooperation rather than conflict and thus lessen the threat of war. . . . Interests will be respected only if it is clear that they can be defended. Restraint will prevail only if its absence is known to carry heavy risks.[11]

While the Nixon and Ford Administrations have consistently placed high confidence in the SALT arms limitations negotiations, their opponents have become increasingly vocal in raising reservations about the procedures, substance and future course of the negotiations.[12] When SALT I became stalemated largely over the issue of the forward based systems, an interim agreement was signed. SALT II successfully resolved the major problem of verification of the quality improvement of the "MIRV-ing" of Soviet ICBM force, but also became deadlocked over the definitions of heavy missiles, heavy bombers, and applicability of the U.S. Cruise missile to the SALT deliberations.

In November 1974 at Vladivostok it was agreed to impose a ceiling of 2400 delivery vehicles for each side, of which 1320 could be MIRV-ed. But subsequent negotiations again became derailed over definitions, and whether and how to include the Soviets Backfire from her and the U.S. Cruise missile. After repeated stalls the Soviets invited Kissinger to visit Moscow in January 1976. A definition was reached for heavy ICBMs which could limit the replacement of the "light" Soviet SS-11 with "heavy" SS-19, thereby restricting the Soviets aggregate throwweight. On the Backfire-Cruise missile issue, the Soviets agreed that bombers could carry 15-20 Cruise missiles and each aircraft would be counted as one unit against the 1320 ceiling for vehicles carrying multiple warheads. They also insisted that Cruise missiles fired from ships be counted against the 2400 total if their

---

[11]Helmut Sonnenfeldt, "The Meaning of Détente," *Naval War College Review*, July-August 1975, pp. 3-8. For a quarter century, he stated, the U.S. was containing a nation that could threaten U.S. interest around the world only ideologically, now it can do so militarily.

[12]cf. Paul H. Nitze, "Nuclear Strategy in an Era of Détente," *Foreign Affairs*, January 1976, for an attack by the most distinguished opponent yet in print of Kissinger's conduct of SALT; on the FBS aspect of SALT I see Joseph Kruzel, "Salt: The Search for a Follow-On Agreement," *Orbis*, Summer 1973.

range exceeded 360 miles. The U.S. side rejected the latter proposal. The Soviets then recommended cutting the total number of vehicles from 2400 to 2100 but would not acknowledge that the Backfire was a strategic bomber.[13] Other constraints on the Backfire must be negotiated.

ROLE OF CONSTRAINTS

There are two basic theoretical reasons for the continuing differences of the two sides over strategic arms limitations. First the U.S. has consistently maintained that the overall objective of arms controls should be the assurance of "crisis stability" and "essential equivalence." These concepts prohibit either opponent from developing a unilateral military advantage by exploiting the mutual understanding that both will be permitted to continue research and development for on-going force modernization. They also offer an alternative formula for pegging security to exact equality in each weapons component, which has had a stimulating effect on arms competition. Both concepts were formulated to provide realistically assured security and ultimately reductions in strategic weapons.

The Soviets have rejected these concepts because of the asymmetrics involved in the two respective geostrategic positions. They have insisted instead on "equal security taking into account geographic and other considerations."[14] Through this conceptualization of security, they resurrected the classical Russian encirclement syndrome. The U.S. is surrounded by friendly states and open oceans. But the USSR is surrounded by potentially hostile threats from China and Europe. Therefore, prudent Soviet security policy requires that Moscow's total forces equal the aggregated strategic nuclear strength of China, France, West Germany, Britain, and the United States. A weaker posture might tempt blackmail or aggression on either or both disparate fronts.[15]

[13]With serious differences between the two sides over Angola, Portugal and the Middle East, the bid to reduce the ceiling did not seriously affect the total Soviet throw-weight which is the determining factor for future weapons developments—the Soviets are probably more inclined now to pursue warhead refinement and accuracy in order to match present U.S. selectivity. Rather the proposal imparted the political connotation of breaking the deadlock and rescuing Ford and Kissinger during an election year when other foreign policy issues were forcing the campaigning to the right. See James Reston's comments, *New York Times*, 22 January 1976.

[14]Nitze, *op.cit.*

[15]In a related context Moscow has continued to promote the idea of an Asian Security Conference as a constraint against China. Peking fears Moscow today, but the

While there is some logic supporting this concept it has been rejected by the U.S. The historic fissures in the West on strategic nuclear policies provide no assurance that all NATO governments will reach a consensus on any response to any given Soviet nuclear challenge. Likewise, the U.S.-Chinese rapprochement has not reached, and is unlikely to do so, the point where joint military operation could be coordinated. Indeed, from the American viewpoint, the prospects for Soviet-Chinese reconciliation in the form of a mutual defense pact vastly outweigh the possibility of any overt Chinese-American military cooperation.

The second fundamental difference also stems from geostratic factors. The Backfire-Cruise Missile issue is a reflection of the geographic asymmetrics involved, which has inadvertently altered the terms of reference at SALT II. Both systems have unlimited range because of aerial refueling capabilities for the Backfire and the multiple-vehicle delivery adaptability of the Cruise missile. Consequently both systems can be employed in either tactical or strategic missions. In the Cruise missile case, if it is mounted on aircraft, submarines and warships, the number of launch platforms for this cheap, accurate, and penetrable system would be limited mainly by the costs for vehicular modifications, which would be much lower than the construction costs for Backfire.

The inclusion of these two "dual-capable" and "dual-roled" systems in the SALT II negotiations when other "forward based systems," such as the U.S. F-111 and the Soviet Medium Range Ballistic Missiles, have been excluded indicates the complexity of the terms of reference problem. The dilemma in categorizing weapons systems was compounded by the apparently politically preferred technique of first establishing numerical ceilings and then attempting to determining what systems they should have included. It is unclear at this point whether the inclusion of some FBS weapons and

---

Soviets are worried about Chinese capabilities in the 1980s. The suspended negotiations over border problems foundered over the rival demands that Soviets experienced in East-West European disputes: reduce military forces before negotiations over political issues can be successful, and a political settlement is a precondition for military disengagement. Unlike the CSCE, an Asian Security Conference could side-step this issue. But the Soviets' chief aim is apparently to try and parallel as closely as possible in the Far East the gains made in CSCE: (1) secure recognition of the territorial status quo, which China, Japan, and others strongly resist; (2) establish military rules of engagement that include adequate insurance against surprise attack that would allow force reductions; (3) generate a new stimulate to trade and exchange of technological information" in the hopes of gaining greater access to the Chinese public.
reasons; and (4) pledge to support, as a last priority, the principle of "freer flow of information, mainly with Japan, that is now lagging for both political and commercial

the exclusion of others will pose serious future problems, or whether it was an inadvertent or deliberate move that underscored the FBS controversy. But it is becoming increasingly clear that the Backfire-Cruise missile confrontation highlights the changing character of SALT II and future strategic arms limitation negotiations.

One of the central issues in all disarmament negotiations up to 1974 was verification. It still is, with the partial exception of strategic delivery vehicles, where both numbers and major quality improvements are detectable by national means of surveillance. The Vladivostok Accord indicated that both sides had high confidence in their respective surveillance capabilities, if allowed to operate without interference.[16] But verification in the Backfire-Cruise missile issue raises new parameters. Bomber aircraft can be physically counted but their intended role cannot be accurately determined because of mobility and refueling factors. Their employment in the strategic role is a matter of political intentions, not physical limitations. The Soviets' refusal to categorize the Backfire as a strategic system suggests that they prefer to keep its employ on unrestricted option.

Verification of the Cruise missile is also a problem of identification and intended employment. Unrestricted deployment of this system on submarines, aircraft, and surface vessels would seriously complicate the Soviet verification problem. Indeed the principles of stability and essential equivalence would probably be violated and renewed arms competition would probably result. This new dimension of the verification issue suggests that the question of physical tabulations and estimates has been surpassed by the more complex factors of determining the capabilities and direction of military research and development and their probable impact on both future force postures and political behavior.

The Cruise Missile case indicates that surveillance and verification techniques do not always match the technological sophistication of new weapons that may be the subjects of future arms negotiations. Without the means for

---

16One of the main problems with verification is that the sensory techniques of both sides have become so refined that it becomes increasingly difficult to distinguish between accurate data and "clutter" or spurious inputs. Both sides reportedly have recognized the danger posed to stability by the collection of inaccurate intelligence and have tacitly agreed not to camouflage, interfere with or deceive each other's sensoring capabilities. The Soviets "blacking-out" of a U.S. surveillance satellite for 18 minutes over the USSR, was apparently a prime reason for the lively discussion in the Winter of 1975 in Washington about the Soviets' violation of the "spirit" of SALT I. *International Herald Tribune*, 16 December 1975, citing an incident on 10 October 1975.

adequate verification for follow-on weapons systems, the process of negotiation based on stability and equivalence rests on political confidence. The military balance is likely to become increasingly sensitive to political atmospheric disturbances. To provide assurances against unilateral bids to gain military advantages in a highly technologized environment, political confidence-building of necessity becomes the underpinning of the "structure of a generation of peace."

This shift of emphasis from technical verification to political confidence is also implied by the "interactionist" school of great power behavioralists. This school perceives stability as the on-going rivalry over mutual suasion and influence competition among third parties. Indeed the rivalry may become more intense as the continually divergent societal aspirations preclude the convergence of political values and motivations[17] Under these circumstances, stability will depend increasingly on political confidence, which the West interprets as a balanced exercise of constraints and the disavowal of attaining unilateral political advantages.

From the Western viewpoint, this consensus is encased in the 1972 Basic Principles that are to govern the special great power relationship. While the overall aim is the self-denial of unilateral quests for advantages, the operative provisions of the Basic Principles deal explicitly and implicitly with the issues of warning, surprise, and duplicity.[18] The Western interpretation is that political confidence and relationship stability prohibit unexpected and potentially uncontrollable moves that might be misperceived as a bid for unilateral gain. Zero sum progressions in interactions require sufficient communications to preclude surprise or the suspicion of deceit.

The first challenge to this concept resulted from the Soviet expulsion from Egypt over the issue of providing "decisive weapons," and the subsequent Soviet decision to fulfill partially Cairo's demands. Soviet involvement in the Arabs' military preparations were so carefully masked that both the U.S. and Israel were convinced that the external powers had been sufficiently dissociated from the Arab-Israeli conflict that hostilities could not erupt. Brezhnev discussed the Middle East situation with Nixon and Kissinger in San Clemente in June 1973, but in such vague terms that he successfully concealed the true situation and yet could later claim that the USSR had

[17]Pierre Hassner, "Europe; Old Conflicts, New Rules," *Orbis*, Fall 1973.

[18]cf. Kissinger's Press Statement in Moscow to this effect, *International Herald Tribune*, 22 January 1976.

complied with the provisions of the Basic Principles, requiring mutual warning of any anticipated increase in international tensions.[19]

Kissinger perceived Soviet behavior as an act of duplicity and launched a major U.S. diplomatic initiative both to promote a durable settlement and to insulate the Middle East crisis from further Soviet manipulation. The subsequent improvement in American-Egyptian relations and the sharp curtailment of Soviet influence in the Arab world apparently led Moscow to conclude that Washington was seeking unilateral advantages in the Middle East that warranted an assertive Soviet policy elsewhere, such as the Indian Ocean and Angola. The seeming violations of the principles of warning and constraint against opportunism and the mutual disregard for the Basic Principles lowered the focus of both sides to the less lofty problems of compliance and enforcement. Political confidence no longer rested on the notion of self-regulation, but reverted to the sounder concept of reciprocity and linkages among negotiable issues and maneuverable levers.[20] Political constraints could no longer be presumed to be an inherent characteristic of the special relationship. Constraints would have to be negotiated or induced. The hopeful distinction with the Cold War era was that constraint could now be fully discussed.

THE NATURE OF THE SPECIAL RELATIONSHIP

It remains now to expand the description of the special great power relationship offered in the first chapter before drawing relevant conclusions. Uwe Nerlich has pointed out that the conceptualization of this relationship has itself undergone distinctive changes in the perspective of both sides.[21] Indeed two separate phases can be identified. The first phase was characterized by the view that the concept imparted profound, sweeping changes in East-West relations. Both the scale and the manner of these dramatic changes were conceived through the perceptual processes and prescribed nothing but transition without definitive end results or objectives. The modifications envisioned substitutional changes in existing structures to provide a more dur-

---

[19]cf. footnote number 2.

[20]The Soviets have continually attempted to compartmentalize both their foreign policy and international negotiations. The U.S. has only occasionally attempted to use non-related issues for leverage (such as Jewish emigration and trade privileges). The Soviets most frequently employed linkage is with the issue of non-discrimination against them (such as most-favored-nation treatment).

[21]Uwe Nerlich, "Beyond Détente," *op. cit.*

able base for "the generation of peace." This dramatic view of the concept prevailed in the 1960s primarily in the West until specific negotiations on security matters provided the evidence for a new perspective—the second phase.

This second view of the interactions holds that they are related to the negotiating process itself and the respective bureaucratic decision-making mechanisms. Greater stress is placed on the continuity and controllability of the negotiation process. Rather than substituting structures, this view requires the creation of complementary structures for existing ones. Nerlich calls the latter perspective the "*consensual* view of détente" and concludes that it is now the prevailing opinion.[22]

The weakness of this understanding of the relationship is that it focuses on the negotiation process and its formal results as ends in themselves and fails to consider the political forces responsible for the bargaining. Furthermore, by stressing newly created structures, such as SALT and MBFR, it omits other, more routinely used, channels for cooperative interactions, such as the 1975 U.S.-Soviet grain transactions. Finally, some of the new structures, (notably CSCE and MBFR) have failed to produce the level of substantive results commensurate with the collective efforts to get them organized. Thus, through both the dramatic conceptualization and the end products of the negotiations high priority became attached to the symbolism inherent in any East-West interaction. This symbolism, in turn, became an end in itself and has added confusion about the true state of the present degree of change taking place in the "abnormal normalization process," to use Egon Bahr's term.

While phase one was characterized by a premature "overselling" of the pentagonal structure of peace, phase two can be seen as a virulent pursuit of negotiations, partly for their own sake, that distorted the limited scope of the bargaining and screened the nature of the interdependence aspect of the relationship. Indeed, a third phase in the understanding of the concept may be emerging wherein symbolism may be minimized and stress may be placed on the accurate prescription of the nature and limits of interdependence.[23]

A central feature of the "dramatic" phase of détente was the rise in Western expectations that a fundamental change was possible in the special

[22]Nerlich, "Beyond Détente," *op. cit.*

[23]*Ibid.* Zbigniew Brzezinski has commented about the options: "The alternative to détente is not war, but a variety of intermediate positions. When there was no détente there was no war either." Interview, *International Herald Tribune*, 26 January 1976.

relationship as evidenced in the "consensual" phase where the concept of continual "cobwebbing" was supposedly reinforcing systemic stability.[24] The difficulty with the "cobwebbing" paradigm, i.e., the creation of a steadily expanding web of agreements that serve as incentives and penalties to insure mutually acceptable behavior, is the question of validation. For example it cannot be decisively demonstrated that more U.S. pressure on the Soviets during Phase Two would have produced greater concessions (as asserted by Kissinger's detractors). It is equally unprovable that the Soviets would have behaved more aggressively or assertively during the "crisis of capitalism" without the constraints of the special relationship. The reason for this validation dilemma is the difficulty in determining the precise value one side attaches to any given interaction or unilateral move, and in insuring that these values will not change unperceived over time. Thus, the effectiveness of the webbing mechanism will remain an accurate reflection of political perceptions of adversary intentions—a task not satisfactorily achieved during phase I and II.[25]

Kissinger's new assertion that the West is facing a permanent "unending challenge" to peace suggests that the nature of interdependence should be reexamined in light of the Soviet view of the development of the international system. The Soviet concept of peaceful coexistence, with its requirements for ideological conflict and increased vigilance, has been superimposed on the special relationship. The Soviets are not likely to yield their abiding faith in the "correlation of historic forces." Their demand for ideological confrontation remains the justification for the doctrine of *Abgrenzung*, or the deliberate filtering of alien values and ideas from penetrating the "Social Commonwealth." And their newly acquired global military capabilities add the dimension of political influence competition now being conducted on a world-wide basis. The combination of these factors indicate that cooperative interdependence has blended with persisting elements of the former adversary confrontation.

[24]John W. Burton, *World Society*, Cambridge University Press, 1972.

[25]At the micro level Kissinger introduced in February 1976 a new intermediate alternative position. If the SALT process falters, the U.S. can be thrust into a new arms build-up that might cost over five years an additional $20 billions. At the macro level of analysis he indicated that changes had occurred in his earlier perception of the special détente, "Today, for the first time in our history, we face the stark reality that the challenge is unending; that there is no easy and surely no final answer; that there are no automatic solutions." Address by Henry A. Kissinger, "The Permanent Challenge to Peace: United States Policy Toward the Soviet Union," before the Commonwealth Club of San Francisco, *USIS Bulletin*, 4 February 1976.

The highest Soviet foreign policy priority still is to manipulate the relationship for the advancement of the "historic forces." Correspondingly the main Western aim is to tame the conflict. The challenge for future relations is to devise concepts that can reliably moderate great power behavior.

One such concept is strategic parity and the logic of its preservation. Rough equivalence in developing military options for possible political actions requires a complementary equivalence in constraints. Neither side has a vital interest in assuming the risks involved in upsetting this delicate balance between options and constraints. Neither power can achieve the ultimate aims held during the stalemate period; yet both can gain minimal goals if expectations are confined to the parameters of mutually acceptable behavior.

A second concept is that of limited or "adversary interdependence and the logic inherent in its perpetuation. The Soviet drive for economic autonomy broke down for a wide variety of reasons and has required massive Western technology transfers to intensify industry and increase productivity. The required "limited opening to the West" has diluted Moscow's promotion of the "historic forces of Socialism" and has induced greater adaptation to pluralism. Furthermore, the desire for some degree of cooperation with the West requires an equivalent degree of responsibility on the Soviet side to insure on-going collaboration at the desired level. Responsible behavior is reinforced by the leverage derived from the linkage between one form of cooperation and another.

A third concept is the impact of systemic multipolarity on great power behavior. The international system is and will remain pluralistic, despite the current interpretation that the "historic forces" will ultimately produce a unitary structure. The respective members of the present system are likely to increasingly seek a more equitable distribution of the entire system's material products. These new demands will tend to standardize the conceptualization of modernity and the modernization process which, in turn, is likely to channel their respective policies increasingly to the interests of the system's other members. The composite character of the system is composed of a multipolar and bipolar chessboard. The competing interests of the great powers in meeting the growing demands of the multipolar world provide ample opportunities to discipline Soviet behavior through the use of normal diplomatic levers.

From the Western viewpoint the perpetuation of these concepts should prescribe a mutually acceptable definition for great power behavior. These concepts permit continued ideological aspirations; yet they also proscribe the most dangerous elements of the rivalry. They do not specify the degree or nature of cooperation; they merely limit the contentions issues and thereby channel the competition.

The deliberate channeling of state interactions away from conflictual issues may be viewed as the pursuit of a *modus vivendi*. While the Soviets are likely to perpetuate their interpretation of systemic development through peaceful coexistence, the West can be expected to shape and mold a *modus vivendi* policy. There appears to be no alternative for the conduct of foreign policy by either side and future great power behavior is likely to be characterized by a moderated or "adversary interdependence."

Index